Quarto is the authority on a wide range of topics.

Quarto educates, entertains and enriches the lives of our readers—enthusiasts and lovers of hands-on living.

www.quartoknows.com

First published in 2016 by Motorbooks, an imprint of Quarto Publishing Group USA Inc., 400 First Avenue North, Suite 400, Minneapolis, MN 55401 USA. Telephone: (612) 344-8100 Fax: (612) 344-8692

quartoknows.com
Visit our blogs at quartoknows.com

Motorbooks titles are also available at discounts in bulk quantity for industrial or sales-promotional use. For details contact the Special Sales Manager at Quarto Publishing Group USA Inc., 400 First Avenue North, Suite 400, Minneapolis, MN 55401 USA.

10 9 8 7 6 5 4 3 2 1

ISBN: 978-0-7603-4604-4

Library of Congress Cataloging-in-Publication Data

Names: Stemp, Marilyn, 1954- author.
Title: Harley-Davidson CVO motorcycles : the motor company's custom vehicle operations / by Marilyn Stemp.
Description: Minneapolis, Minnesota : Quarto Publishing Group USA Inc., Motorbooks, 2015.
Identifiers: LCCN 2015036633 | ISBN 9780760346044 (hardcover)
Subjects: LCSH: Harley-Davidson motorcycle--History.
Classification: LCC TL448.H3 S738 2015 | DDC 629.227/5--dc23
LC record available at http://lccn.loc.gov/2015036633

Acquiring Editor: Darwin Holmstrom
Project Manager: Jordan Wiklund
Art Director: Brad Springer
Cover Designer: Simon Larkin
Layout: Karl Laun

Printed in China

HARLEY-DAVIDSON®

CVO™

MOTORCYCLES

CONTENTS

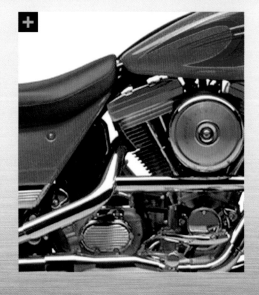

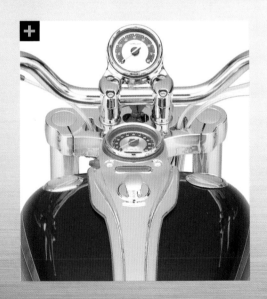

INTRODUCTION

A collection of rare CVO motorcycles looking for new horizons.

Dreams. No matter where we are in our motorcycling experience, dreams drive us towards our goals. Asleep or awake, the future we imagine and hope for motivates us through the course of our lives. The dream of building custom motorcycles drives us to attack a fender with a hacksaw, just as the dream of owning a Harley-Davidson motorcycle can help us kick start a ragged moped in the quest to taste two-wheeled freedom.

RIGHT:
Special techniques, graphics, and finishes
are just part of the formula.

BELOW:
A CVO motorcycle and the open road:
what more could you want?

These dreams compose the very fiber from which Custom Vehicle Operations motorcycles are woven. As the premier custom machines from the world's premier motorcycle manufacturer, a Harley-Davidson CVO motorcycle blends individual detail with legendary presence. When the CVO motorcycle program was born with the unveiling of the 1999 FXR[2] and FXR[3] motorcycles, it fulfilled the dream of a dedicated core group of riders who wanted nothing more than a new FXR. As the program grew and its range expanded, the mission stayed the same: fulfilling dreams through the experience of motorcycling.

A relatively recent branch of the generations-old Harley-Davidson Motor Company, the Custom Vehicle Operations department is built on a legacy of modification that's almost as old as Harley-Davidson itself. More than a century ago Harley-Davidson offered its first parts and accessories catalog, establishing a tradition of individualization that was unique in motorcycling. Harley-Davidson motorcycles have seen every type of modification, from swapping fenders to swapping heads, engines, and everything in between.

It was a pattern that the factory couldn't fail to see. When Willie G. and his team unveiled the Super Glide motorcycle in 1971, factory customization hit the big time. Now, anyone could speak their mind through the medium of the motorcycle; it didn't take a lifetime of trial and error to have a beautiful, unique piece of two-wheeled art. Without diminishing the value of truly one-off and specialized machines, Harley had made it possible for riders the world over to express themselves through their motorcycles.

Soon factory customs were rampant in the Harley-Davidson model lineup. Motorcycles like the FXDB Sturgis and FLSTS Heritage Springer Softail proved that

ABOVE TOP:
Even your hands will know that this is a custom machine.

ABOVE BOTTOM:
Project Rushmore put a strong focus on ergonomic hand controls and buttons.

LEFT:
Let no one doubt where your machine comes from!

Just a one-finger push brings the gas cap to hand for luxury and elegance found on no other motorcycle.

a motorcycle with a unique blend of parts and a factory warranty was something the public wanted, and wanted badly. The chance to unleash more defined and directed creativity within Harley-Davidson came about first by happenstance, when production was discontinued on the military-spec MT500, leaving the Special Operations Group building at the York, Pennsylvania, factory without a purpose. This void would soon find new life as the home of the budding CVO motorcycle group. When the first FXR[2] and FXR[3] models initially took shape on the small-volume production line in 1998, a spark ignited brilliant synergy between time, place and opportunity.

Each CVO model represents the highest standard to which a factory custom can be built. The choice of platforms that receive the treatment varies from year to year, but the results consistently represent the pinnacle of design, power, and technology for a given point in Harley-Davidson's history. This is no surprise to fans of the Motor Company; no rider on the planet would forgo the chance of owning their dream bike. Such is the power of dreams in this splendid sport, culture, and lifestyle we call motorcycling.

Join us as we explore the history of Harley-Davidson CVO motorcycles, from the first handsome FXR models to the catalog-topping dream machines the CVO motorcycle team turns out today. Stay the course, turn the page, and enjoy the ride!

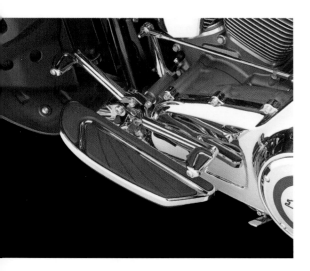

Custom controls add traction and control with a unique touch.

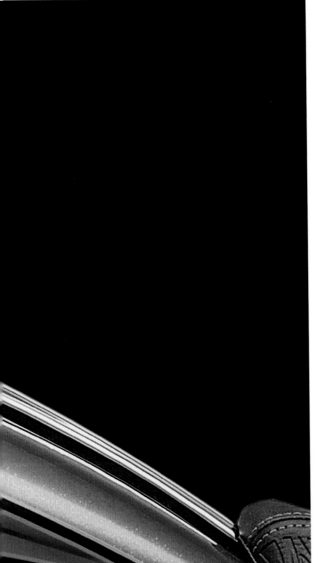

ABOVE:
No CVO motorcycle would be complete
without a dip into the Screamin' Eagle
performance catalogue.

CHAPTER 1

Arresting Red Pearl was one of the color options for the original FXR² motorcycle.

HARLEY-DAVIDSON
FXR:
THE FIRST
CVO MODELS

FXR MODELS: THE ORIGIN

The outstanding handling attributes of Harley-Davidson's FXR models were once only appreciated by motorcycling's most enlightened riders. Though the cult status these models enjoy today was not so firmly established in the late 1990s, the buzz among fans touting the FXR model's superior riding characteristics began at that time, both in and out of V-twin circles. It actually began much earlier, in the late 1980s. Today, the FXR motorcycle is still regarded among purists as the best-handling Harley-Davidson motorcycle ever.

TOP:
The FXR chassis dates back to the Shovelhead era.

ABOVE RIGHT:
The FXLR Low Rider model was loaded with custom details, foreshadowing the CVO motorcycle line.

ABOVE:
The bike that started it all: the FXR^2 motorcycle.

From its introduction in 1982, the media has touted the FXR motorcycle as "the engineer's bike" and praised its responsive ride. The model also showcased breakthrough styling that both demanded and withstood scrutiny. Charles Plueddeman wrote in the October 25, 2010, issue of *Hot Bike* that

> the FXR does represent a moment in Harley history when the company put its talent and energy into creating not just a great Harley-Davidson, but a great motorcycle; a bike less constrained by heritage and the status quo . . . . The FXR represented Harley's commitment to its future.

When FXR motorcycle production ended in 1994, the model had become the favorite platform of custom builders, a position that solidified its iconic status. And it's this element—the FXR solid position in the evolution of V-twin motorcycling—that also made it the logical foundation for Harley-Davidson's initial experiment in limited-edition, custom-designed production motorcycles. The FXR motorcycle provided the platform for the Harley-Davidson Motor Company's very first Custom Vehicle Operations (CVO) models.

The FXR^2 and FXR^3 models were released in 1999. Jim Hofman, who retired in 2014 after heading up the CVO division for years, was working in the Parts & Accessories Division when the first CVO models were released. "The original idea behind CVO was simple," he explained. "To leverage the creative expertise of Willie G. and his styling team, and to combine the large array of H-D's Genuine Accessories with the talent within H-D to build limited production, highly accessorized, custom vehicles."

As a favorite of the motorcycle press, motor corps officers, customizers, and certain traditionalist H-D customers and certain 1%ers, the FXR motorcycle seemed like a natural choice for Harley-Davidson's first factory custom. But choosing it for this experiment in limited production customs was a practical decision, not an emotional one.

Consider where Harley-Davidson and Harley motorcycle riders were at the time. The 1990s enjoyed a healthy economy, and the motorcycle industry was thriving due to significant mainstream attention. Waiting lists were common at dealerships. According to a contemporary *Chicago Tribune* article, by 1996 Harley-Davidson was producing nearly three times as many motorcycles as it had a dozen years before, and the company had a up to two-year backlog of orders. H-D's reputation for quality was solid, its bikes sold at a premium, and demand for them was intense.

Later in the decade, the marketplace lost track of Harley's R&D efforts, which centered on developing the groundbreaking twin cam engine; for their part, the company wasn't quite ready to reveal it. But motorcycle riders wanted Harley motorcycles, and finding supply to fill that demand was paramount.

According to Hofman, the idea of building limited-production, high-end, factory custom motorcycles germinated within the Parts & Accessories Division, aided by the serendipitous availability of a small specialty production line from the York, Pennsylvania, factory. The manufacturing arm of the company was already working flat out, and, though the factory custom idea had appeal, assembly line time and excess parts were unavailable for a pilot custom production effort.

Building 42 at H-D's facility in York was a special operations area where teams of skilled craftsmen hand-assembled limited production runs of certain race and military machines, such as the VR1000 race bike and MT 500 for military use. When a military contract ended in the 1990s, it made room for something new to take over the space: the timing was right for something custom.

The group got together with then-vice president of Parts & Accessories, Ron Hutchinson, and agreed that they saw an opportunity. Everyone agreed: "We have people. We have a building. Let's do something."

The other FXR^2 color option was Stone Cold Blue.

Harley-Davidson followed the FXR[2] model with the FXR[3] model.

"Hutch was a strong leader and a visionary," said Hofman. "He convinced (CEO Jeff) Bleustein it would work." The new program would not be part of original equipment engineering or mainstream manufacturing—it would operate separately.

With that point established, another question came up. "What can we build that people will love without disrupting regular production?" said Hofman. "We soon realized the FXR motorcycle had unique parts; it would not collide with manufacturing and the tooling was on hand."

Of course, in 1999, the term "custom vehicle operations" had not yet been coined and, in fact, the project was considered only a one-time effort. According to Hofman, "when we first started out we thought this FXR project was the beginning *and* the end. We had no idea how popular it would be."

When the Road Glide motorcycle joined the FXR4 motorcycle for limited custom production the following year (2000), it donned a plethora of components from H-D's Screamin' Eagle line of performance parts, bringing with it the expectation that, from this point forward, these motorcycles would excel not only in astonishing good looks but in power and performance as well.

Harley-Davidson recognized that their customers had a strong penchant for customizing and personalizing their motorcycles. Components from the company's Parts & Accessories Division sold well, and new designs were regularly introduced; this is an important part of the story of the CVO models.

Sure, exclusivity is one aspect in the allure of limited production custom motorcycles, but another factor is the ability of such models to inspire and motivate other owners. The CVO model represents just one way for an owner to customize a stock bike, but the possibilities are abundant and nearly infinite. In fact, many CVO motorcycle owners customize these dynamic beauties still further after purchase.

Harley-Davidson built 620 Emerald Green Metallic FXR[3] models but produced just 64 in Blue Flame, shown here.

The Motor Company used a bolder graphic treatment on the FXR[4] motorcycle rather than the understated graphics of the FXR[2] and FXR[3] motorcycles.

As time went on and more models entered the factory custom program, Screamin' Eagle components became a mainstay, so people started adding the Screamin' Eagle name to these models until it stuck. Though the division had taken on the designation "CVO" a few years earlier, by 2009 it was officially added to model names.

THE DETAILS

So far we've covered the history of H-D's FXR line. Next, let's get back to the details of those first FXR limited production models. The two versions produced in 1999, labeled FXR^2 and FXR^3, had black-and-chrome, 1340cc Evolution engines. The FXR^2 model came with a 21-inch laced front wheel and the FXR^3 model had a 19-inch cast front wheel. Paint jobs then weren't nearly as elaborate as those seen on today's CVO models. The 2 was offered in either Arresting Red or Stone Cold Blue. The 3 stepped it up with a two-tone flame paint scheme in either Candy Emerald Green or Bright/Dark Candy Blue.

Those who have studied the subject say the FXR^2 and FXR^3 models are mechanically identical to the 1994 production model FXR, except for a new wiring harness with updated connectors, an updated nine-plate clutch, and a vacuum-operated fuel valve.

Dipping into the H-D P&A Genuine Motor Accessories catalog netted dozens of shiny parts for the FXR^2 model, carefully chosen for the best effect. The handlebars and all the controls, levers, and covers on the bars are chrome accessories, finishing up with chrome-and-rubber Horizontal Handlebar Grips and Oval Bar & Shield Billet-Style Mirrors. Chrome trim panels, nut and bolt covers, inserts, and covers abound.

The FXR^3 motorcycle had all that, plus a new custom front fender and custom side covers. To coordinate with the ThunderStar™ Five-Spoke Cast Wheels (19-inch front and 16-inch rear), there's a matching, chrome five-spoke Rear Belt Sprocket and chrome Floating Brake Disc, front and rear. A special custom-style seat and passenger backrest addressed comfort. An easy way to recognize the FXR^3 motorcycle? The two-tone paint is the giveaway.

When the FXR^4 motorcycle was released in 2000, it was the year's only motorcycle in the H-D lineup with the vaunted Evo powerplant, once called "the engine that saved Harley-Davidson." The new twin cam, released in 1999, was incorporated into the remaining Big Twin production models in 2000. So the FXR motorcycle and the Evo engine rolled proudly into H-D history together in provocative and memorable fashion, silver powder-coated cases.

The FXR^4 motorcycle's 19-inch laced front wheel was paired with a solid chrome rear wheel. A new seat and Chrome Drag Bars were added. Updates over the 1999 FXR motorcycle included sealed wheel bearings, a sealed battery, dual 4-piston calipers, shocks from P&A, and an electronic speedometer. Brilliant eye candy arrived in the form of additional chrome pieces along with billet components such as mirrors, footpegs, shifter peg, and grips. Paint and graphics hit the mark with two options: Screaming Yellow Pearl with Eclipse Graphics or Candy Tangerine with Eclipse Graphics.

There's no doubt: the three limited edition FXR models of 1999 and 2000 put a stake in the ground to establish today's dynamic CVO motorcycle program. These inaugural models set the pace to inform both Harley motorcycle riders and Harley brass of the spark that ignites and the unexpected opportunities that appear when creativity meets innovation. Even in those two short years, it became clear that, not only was Harley-Davidson capable of producing factory custom motorcycles, but there were indeed eager customers impatiently waiting to buy and ride them. And that's still true.

The FXR[4] motorcycle marked the end of the line for the beloved FXR chassis as well as for the Evolution engine.

CHAPTER

This 2002 Screamin' Eagle Road King motorcycle sports Candy Brandywine Radical paint with contrasting flames.

TOURING MOTORCYCLES: CVO

MOTORCYCLES FOR THE LONG HAUL

FLHRSE1 SCREAMIN' EAGLE ROAD KING MOTORCYCLE

The Harley-Davidson Road King motorcycle has it all: classic good looks, roadworthy performance, and high-profile genealogy. It's a versatile, adrenaline-pumping motorcycle that's as capable of running over to bike night as it is running over the Rockies. And this reputation isn't mere illusion, since the Road King motorcycle can trace its lineage back to Harley-Davidson's storied mid-century decades when the intrepid motorcycle rider chased the sunset with only a sense of adventure as companion.

The other livery offered on the 2002 Screamin' Eagle Road King motorcycle was Purple Radical with silver flames.

In those days, before full dressers were as prevalent as they are now, there was the FLHS Electra Glide Sport motorcycle, a slimmed-down version of the FLH Electra Glide motorcycle, with no fairing or Tour-Pak luggage. The Sport had two runs—from 1979 to 1982 and again from 1987 to 1993. When the Road King motorcycle appeared in 1994, it effectively replaced the Electra Glide Sport motorcycle, and it's been a perennially popular model in the Harley-Davidson lineup ever since.

Road King motorcycles have performance prominence and a flexible orientation. They're viewed as a motorcycle that fills the gap between full dresser and cruiser , retaining the best qualities of each. Another sign of how the Road King motorcycle rules? It's been tagged to be a CVO model *six* times. Make no mistake: with its first appearance as a factory custom model in 2002, the Screamin' Eagle Road King motorcycle was a consequential advancement in the development of the CVO motorcycle program. Its introduction and continued inclusion as a CVO model planted the seeds for later Street Glide and Electra Glide CVO models.

In 2002, just the fourth year of Harley-Davidson's factory custom program, the CVO motorcycle group had built not only exceptional motorcycles but high expectations and demand as well. So when the Road King motorcycle, an already widely praised motorcycle, was pumped up with a silver-and-chrome Twin Cam 95 engine to become the first-ever limited edition Road King motorcycle, the bike quickly took pride of place as the darling of the touring crowd. The vibration-isolation mounted engine touted a bore and stroke of 3.87 by 4.0 and featured pushrod-operated overhead valves with hydraulic self-adjusting lifters. A heftier 1.4-kilowatt starter coaxed the 3.9-inch pistons into action. Responsive throttle control came courtesy of electronic sequential port fuel injection, while integrated cruise control and a custom leather seat ensured that the sum of the parts would certainly impress. The FLHRSE1 came

ABOVE:
CVO models come in bold and handsome color schemes, but they all receive the same hand-finished paintwork.

LEFT:
Harley-Davidson celebrated its centennial by offering the 2003 Screamin' Eagle Road King motorcycle in this Centennial Gold livery.

Harley-Davidson offered the 2007 Screamin' Eagle Road King Classic motorcycle in Razor Red with Burnt Gold Leaf graphics.

in two color options and relatively small numbers: just over 400 in Brandywine with Flames, and about 1,700 in Purple with Flames.

For the 2003 hundredth anniversary of Harley-Davidson, further refinements were conferred on the Road King motorcycle by the factory custom team along with several groundbreaking elements, foremost among them a 103 cubic inch motor. This was the first Harley-Davidson model to be so equipped. And staking its claim as a true, ground-up custom, the 2003 Screamin' Eagle Road King motorcycle featured a powder-coated frame, the first of any H-D touring model. Eclipsing even these significant characteristics is the paint treatment. Looking to emulate but not duplicate the 100th Anniversary theme, the CVO model's paint and graphics artists developed just one intricate design, in Centennial Gold with Black and Ripped Burgundy Accents for the fender, tank, side covers, and saddlebags. Broken spears of color seem to tear through the panels, emphasized with hand-painted pinstripes applied at Harley-Davidson's Tomahawk facility. More remarkably, a dozen H-D employees at Tomahawk were taught how to hand-pinstripe, specifically to paint the 2003 Screamin' Eagle Road King motorcycle!

Other notable features are the hydraulically actuated high-performance clutch, hefty final belt drive, spun-aluminum, solid wheels, Stratum collection chrome accessories, and the exclusive hundredth anniversary badges unique to this year, and *only* this year.

These enhancements to the 2002 and 2003 Road King motorcycles were essentially gilding the lily: the Road King motorcycle was perfectly pleasing and compellingly competent in stock trim. But one of the goals of CVO motorcycle team has been to set an example for how to make a great motorcycle even better. For this reason, after a three-year hiatus, the Road King motorcycle once again came under scrutiny. And why not? Plenty had happened in the interim.

The 2007 Screamin' Eagle Road King Classic motorcycle was also available in Black Ice with Pewter Leaf graphics.

Most noticeably, the 2007 FLHRSE proved that old adage, "there's no replacement for displacement." The '07 CVO Road King motorcycle was favored with a 110 cubic inch black-and-chrome twin cam engine, new to CVO models in that year. The six-speed Cruise Drive transmission engaged new chromed Road Winder forged aluminum wheels: an 18-inch by 3.5-inch up front covered by a Fat Boy-style fender, and a 17-inch by 4.5-inch in the rear sporting a wider fender graced by a retro tombstone taillight.

The Road King motorcycle was upgraded for the long haul that year with leather saddlebags, featuring raised flames on the lids and a matching two-up seat with adjustable and detachable backrests for rider and passenger. Adding both comfort and pizzazz are a slew of parts from the H-D Parts & Accessories Ironside Collection,

The third color option for the 2007 Screamin' Eagle Road King Classic motorcycle was Candy Cobalt with Pale Gold Leaf graphics.

The CVO Road King motorcycle is a modern twist on a classic theme.

such as grips, rider footboard inserts, passenger footpegs, shifter peg, brake pedal pad, and more. A flush-mount gas cap and backlit gauges with spun aluminum faces are details CVO motorcycle owners expect..

The three lavish paint options for 2007 left no doubt about the lineage of these motorcycles. They are: Razor Red with Burnt Gold Leaf Graphics; Candy Cobalt with Pale Gold Leaf Graphics; and Black Ice with Pewter Leaf Graphics.

When the Road King motorcycle again appeared in the CVO lineup in 2008, it was to celebrate Harley-Davidson's 105th Anniversary year, sporting cutting-edge metal treatment styling. The 110 Twin Cam received granite-and-chrome finishing, a process that employs special gray paint mixed with stainless steel flakes. Crystal Copper and Black Onyx coloring for the 105th was just one of three paint combinations offered for CVO Road King motorcycle buyers: also available were Black Diamond and Silver Dust with Ghost Flames; and Twilight Blue and Candy Cobalt with Ghost Flames.

Putting looks aside—as if that's possible with *any* CVO model—engineering raised the stakes in 2008 with innovations that not only improve ride quality, but also addressed appearance. First is electronic throttle control (ETC), an ECU-controlled throttle system that works with sequential port fuel injection to improve throttle response. *Thunder Press*'s Terry Roorda offered this description: "It's an elegant

setup, and not only does it eliminate the maintenance, adjustment, and operational vagaries of a mechanical throttle, it optimizes motor performance and provides an unprecedented smoothness in throttle operation and response." It also interfaces seamlessly with the electronic cruise control that's already a feature on the Road King motorcycle. And because the wires run inside the handlebars, front-end clutter is reduced for a more sanitary look.

This change backed into another engineering accomplishment: the addition of an anti-lock braking system (ABS). Though not entirely new to Harley-Davidson motorcycles, the version of ABS on CVO motorcycles is well integrated so it does not take away from the motorcycle's styling cues. Parts of the system are in the wheel bearing and axle spacer while the ABS module slips in under the right side cover. That space was previously home to the cruise control unit so, as Roorda explains,

> To overcome that obstacle, the designers decided that the cruise control module would have to be eliminated, and the only way to do that was to make the thing a peripheral circuit of the fuel injection control unit. And all they had to do to effect that change was to eliminate the throttle cable.

"CVO" means blending history with motorcycling's cutting edge.

And that completes the circle back to ETC and the ECU-controlled throttle system.

Also in 2008, CVO Motorcycle Group added an isolation drive system to Road King models, an innovation borrowed from V-Rod motorcycle technology that makes for smoother, quieter shifting. Other upgrades include Brembo brake components for super stopping with a lighter pull, a new six-gallon fuel tank, and a full FL-style front fender.

Once again, the Road King motorcycle took a break from the CVO roster after two consecutive years. Is there a pattern here? And it was coincidentally *another* anniversary that signaled its return. Harley-Davidson's 110th celebration in 2013 and a celebratory paint scheme once again led the way. Diamond Dust and Obsidian with Palladium Graphics, the featured styling for H-D's 110th Anniversary, was joined by Burgundy Blaze with Hot Fusion Graphics and Crushed Sapphire with Cold Fusion Graphics. Due to a new, multi-step process of hand-finished graphics created with textures and solvents, each paint set is unique. They are simply stunning, every single one!

A few years before, in 2009, the OE Road King motorcycle debuted a new frame that had been re-designed for the rigors of long haul touring. It was carried forward from that time, especially benefitting the 2013 CVO Road King motorcyle with its powerful 110 cubic inch engine, the largest displacement V-twin ever offered by Harley-Davidson. Also on board: ABS, electronic cruise control, and the Assist & Slip Clutch Pack to reduce engine load on downshifts. Addressing the Road King motorcycle's slammed, badass looks there are Agitator custom wheels, a low-profile chrome instrument console, extended saddlebags, and Slipstream Collection controls from hand to foot.

Sure, Road King motorcycles are known for their road-ready, stripped-down posture, but the product development people at Harley-Davidson know that even hot-rodders like their road tunes. So a marked addition for the 2013 CVO Road King motorcycle is the first-ever factory-installed audio system on the model. Its four speakers, 200-watt amplifier, and iPod interface are controlled from the handlebars: crank it up and the miles melt away. Also enabling longer saddle time is the addition of fairing lowers and a new adjustable and detachable Vented Wind Splitter windshield, which almost seems to float over the front end.

If past is prologue, then, of course the Road King motorcycle performed an encore in 2014 for its sixth appearance as a CVO model. While this year coincidentally marked the Road King motorcycle's twentieth anniversary, it was also quite a momentous moment for Harley-Davidson with the company's introduction of Project Rushmore. According to a press release, Project Rushmore was the largest scale new model launch in H-D's history, encompassing "eight new motorcycles that feature improved power and braking performance, enhanced rider ergonomics, and dramatic styling updates that completely redefine and fundamentally transform the touring motorcyclist's experience." Project Rushmore stopped motorcycling in its tracks worldwide—and if you don't think that's worth pursuing, you're not a genuine Harley motorcycle rider!

Project Rushmore enhancements were revealed in upgrades such as the new Reflex Linked Brakes with ABS, Daymaker LED lighting front and rear, and a new steering head with stiffer front forks. These and other significant changes, such as ergonomically designed hand controls with improved feel, were met with acclaim across the board.

Harley-Davidson called this livery Deep Sherwood Pearl and Galactic Black with Aztec Shadow graphics.

ABOVE:

The read end of a pure custom bagger, with fit and finish only the factory can provide.

ABOVE RIGHT:

The 2014 CVO Road King model was reshaped in a wind tunnel for better airflow.

Several advancements in both form and function are specific to the 2014 CVO Road King model. There are hot-rod touchstones such as the Heavy Breather air cleaner, color matched fork sliders, "tuck and roll" leather seat, and stretched saddlebags with One-Touch latches. The blacked-out frame and driveline components take their cue from the 2013 110th Anniversary Edition CVO Road King motorcycle, advancing the design further with blacked-out handlebars, engine guard, and accessories. Mirror Chrome Agitator custom wheels and a new low-profile front fender point the way to serendipity.

As you'd expect, the '14 Road King motorcycle retains the 110 Twin Cam engine, mated to a six-speed Cruise Drive transmission and nestled in the stoutly engineered H-D Touring chassis. The popular Vented Wind Splitter windshield introduced in 2013 returns along with the Assist & Slip Clutch Pack with its reduced-effort lever.

Clearly, every aspect of the riding experience has been probed and considered to surpass any need or expectation. You might say that's appropriate for a motorcycle of this caliber, but the 2014 factory custom Road King motorcycle is a compelling machine even by the uncompromising standards of the CVO motorcycle team.

And, speaking of staunch requirements, paint and graphics artists have stepped up their game, too, bringing multilayered visuals and textures to the '14 CVO Road King motorcycle. Color options are: Deep Sherwood Pearl and Galactic Black with Aztec Shadow Graphics; Titanium Dust and Galactic Black with Aztec Shadow Graphics; and Tribal Orange and Galactic Black with Aztec Shadow Graphics.

And so the Road King motorcycle abides, anchoring a significant place in H-D model history. But more than that: if you ask a non-rider to picture a classic Harley-Davidson cruiser, many will conjure up a motorcycle that looks much like those pictured here, motorcycles that combine nostalgic styling cues with contemporary capability. And that's by design. That's the CVO Road King motorcycle: elegant, powerful, and quintessentially Harley-Davidson.

The tank badge on the 2013 CVO Road King motorcycle celebrated the Motor Company's 110th anniversary.

Harley-Davidson named this color combination Burgundy Blaze with Hot Fusion graphics.

FLHTCSE SCREAMIN' EAGLE ELECTRA GLIDE MODEL

Harley-Davidson Touring bikes have come a long way since the dawn of motorcycling, when the only difference between a touring and cruiser was how far and how fast you rode it. Unique among modern motorcycle companies, the Motor Company has been with us for the whole evolution of the machine, having built virtually every kind of motorcycle that's ever rolled off an assembly line. But, decade after decade, it became obvious that motorcycles made uniquely good tools for one task more than others: getting out on the road, seeing the world, and seeking whatever the rider could find over the next horizon.

For generations, Harley-Davidson has provided the mounts for these long-haul adventures. The heritage of the Touring motorcycles that we now know today began with the introduction of the FL series in 1941, in the midst of wartime production.

While this meant the model received little initial attention, the concept would build up quite a head of steam. Harley FL motorcycles would become world-renowned, selling in record-breaking numbers over the years and carrying riders across roads on every continent of the globe.

The first Harley-Davidson model to wear the Electra Glide moniker arrived in 1965, replacing the Duo-Glide model and sporting a 12-volt charging system with electric starter. The fundamental layout was so strong that the Electra Glide motorcycle soldiered on through the best and worst periods at Harley-Davidson, including the AMF years, competition from foreign makes, and the triumphal introduction of the Evolution powerplant. By the mid-1990s, the Electra Glide motorcycle became the first production Harley-Davidson motorcycle to be offered with fuel injection; a decade later, the model still sat at the top of the heap as the most capable and fully featured motorcycle the Motor Company offered.

Improving on such a steadily refined and perfected motorcycle wasn't going to be easy, but the CVO motorcycle team never signed up for easy! So the team set out to highlight the Electra Glide motorcycle's starring role in Harley-Davidson history after nearly a half-century of production in 2004 with the FLHTCSE Screamin' Eagle Electra Glide motorcycle. It debuted as the ultimate, grand American tourer loaded with the luxury and exclusivity that make CVO models shine so bright among their already-impressive stock brethren.

Harley-Davidson offered the 2004 Screamin' Eagle Electra Glide motorcycle in one of two paint schemes: Candy Cobalt and Starlight Black, shown here.

The other color combination that Harley-Davidson offered for the 2004 Screamin' Eagle Electra Glide motorcycle was Orange Pearl and Jet Black.

But the Screamin' Eagle Electra Glide motorcycle is more than an all-out accessory festival: it serves as a spiritual link between the full-tour dressers roaming the highways today and the original Hydra-Glide, Duo-Glide, and Electra Glide models of the 1940s, 1950s, and 1960s. To the modern eye, it looks almost like a Street Glide motorcycle with its batwing fairing and tapered, uncluttered profile, but the Street Glide motorcycle, popular as it is now, was still just a twinkle in Willie G.'s eye when the FLHTCSE hit the scene. This is just one more example of how the CVO motorcycle group has been such a force for Harley-Davidson, pushing boundaries and forging the future of the brand with its enduring, groundbreaking creations.

The link between this fine machine and its forebears goes beyond its handsome profile and timeless lines. Just take a look at the crown jewel nestled in the frame: a specially tuned, 103 cubic inch twin cam "stroker," sporting the handsome 45-degree split that's become an icon of American motorcycling. Viewed next to the Knucklehead and Panhead motors of the early FLs, it's easy to see how the heritage has been preserved, even as fuel delivery, refinement, and power have been updated for a new millennium. Handsomely finished in silver and chrome, the FHTCSE's stroked twin cam, like the Big Twins of yore, is all about torque! So much torque, in fact, that it has an up-rated starter motor to crank the big beast to life.

Harley-Davidson has always known the value of long-stroke, single-crank pin engines: easy cruising, natural clutch take-up, and that pleasing "potato-potato" exhaust note at idle that turns into a fearsome roar near redline. But the stroked 103 doesn't give up any of the refinement that makes a Harley FL motorcycle such a nice place to spend the day; according to *Motorcycle Cruiser* magazine, "The upsized engine has done nothing to degrade the good road manners of the basic Electra Glide motorcycle. It's still as smooth as a tourer should be." That blend of performance and luxury has been there since the beginning, but leave it to the CVO motorcycle team to take it one step further.

Of course, attention to detail and history can be seen from fender to fender on this machine, making it a rare and beautiful beast among the pleasing but numerous OE Electra Glide motorcycles to roll out of Milwaukee over the past decades. Some details are easy to spot: take the custom three-spoke "Detonator" wheels, 16 inches at both ends and contrast-finished for added flair. No one will be surprised to learn that the two color schemes were exclusive for this machine: Candy Cobalt and Starlight Black being the understated choice while Orange Pearl and Jet Black proudly represents the combination we know so well.

The 2005 Screamin' Eagle Electra Glide motorcycle was available in one of three two-toned color schemes. This one was called Light Candy Cherry and Dark Candy Cherry.

A 2005 Screamin' Eagle Electra Glide motorcycle in Light Candy Teal and Dark Candy Teal
(top), and Stingray Silver (opposite).

Other details include custom color-matched pieces, like the fairing lowers with
added glove boxes, painted inner fairing, and side covers for a coherent custom look
that's almost impossible to replicate in the aftermarket. And if you love chrome, you're
in luck. The Screamin' Eagle Electra Glide motorcycle has a healthy helping of both
cosmetic and functional parts, like the voltage regulator, oil cooler cover, oil filter
mount, axle covers, fork covers, and nearly every bracket and mount you can lay your
eyes on. When the sun comes out, your friends better have their shades on!

The fairing gets more than a modicum of attention, too, with spun aluminum faces
on its full complement of instruments, plus a cut-down, custom-tinted windscreen and
a powerful stereo with integrated amp and CD player, with the speakers right in the
fairing. Grip the chrome bars and you'll notice the clean internal wiring—an impressive
feat in its own right—with features like cruise control available at the bar switches.
Other amenities include custom floorboards for the rider and passenger, plus backrests for both spots on the custom leather seat.

All this luxury is kept in check by a platform that's enjoyed careful development
over five decades, from the air-adjustable rear shocks to the triple brake calipers with
"Detonator" rotors to match the handsome wheels. Comfort is king on the long haul,
so the carefully formed FL frame contains provisions for rubber-mounting the drivetrain,
offering less vibration and more comfort while wringing out that big twin cam stroker.

The Screamin' Eagle Electra Glide motorcycle stayed on the books for another

year, giving buyers one more chance to enjoy this classic blend of craftsmanship, heritage, and power. The 2005 Screamin' Eagle Electra Glide motorcycle featured a few tweaks to keep the bike exclusive without diluting the fundamental balance of the machine. The seat was reshaped and received custom-stitched leather inserts, while a host of Stealth collection accessories set the new edition apart. Wheels and paint schemes received their due attention, resulting in striking new ThunderStar rolling stock finished in chrome with matching brake rotors. Three different color combinations were on offer for '05: Sunrise Yellow Pearl and Stingray Silver; Two-Tone Candy Cherry; and Two-Tone Candy Teal all joined the CVO design pallet. And that would be the end of the story for the Screamin' Eagle Electra Glide motorcycle, slated to stand down for the new '06 Screamin' Eagle Ultra Classic motorcycle that would carry the torch into the next decade.

As one of the earliest FL models to receive the CVO model treatment, the Screamin' Eagle Electra Glide motorcycle both represented the past and pointed towards the future: the next decade of CVO motorcycle production would see the iconic FL variants go from high-powered cruisers to full-bore custom baggers capable of taking on any scene or highway. Perched between the history of Harley-Davidson touring bikes and the current boom in custom baggers, the Screamin' Eagle Electra Glide motorcycle remains one of the most desirable CVO models, even ten years on. Heritage, power, and craftsmanship: it's a Harley-Davidson motorcycle, through and through.

For 2005 gave the Screamin' Eagle Elecra Glide motorcycle a reshaped seat with custom-stitched leather inserts.

FLHTCUSE SCREAMIN' EAGLE ULTRA CLASSIC ELECTRA GLIDE MOTORCYCLE

Staying power: it's been Harley-Davidson's unspoken mantra for more than a century. Either here or abroad, few companies have endured as Harley-Davidson has. From humble beginnings, through world wars, tariff battles, and buyouts, H-D has exhibited rare grit and determination that's as strong in the company's DNA as it is in the motorcycles they build. Take the FL series, which has been around since 1941 and shows no signs of losing its appeal. In light of the contemporary taste for baggers, FLs are set to be a big part of Harley's world for years to come.

But what does staying power have to do with CVO models? Truth is, the CVO branch is the new kid on the block in Harley-Davidson's long history, and, since CVO models' inception, bikes in the program have been limited-production, smaller-run machines. But in this world of trimmed model runs, brief bursts of production, and exclusive, one-year-only options, there is a CVO model that exemplifies the persistence of the brand itself: the Screamin' Eagle Ultra Classic Electra Glide motorcycle.

Boasting both the longest production run as well as the longest *title* in the glittering world of CVO motorcycles, the FLHTCUSE represents the breakout album of the Custom Vehicle Operations: it's like *Who's Next*, *Led Zeppelin IV*, and *Let it Bleed* rolled into a fire-breathing beast of chrome and steel. You just can't help coming back to it, no matter how many times you've heard it.

Produced from 2006 to 2013, the Screamin' Eagle Ultra Classic motorcycle was a spin-off from the popularity of the Screamin' Eagle Electra Glide motorcycle, built for two short years in 2004 and 2005. The model proved so popular that the CVO motorcycle team was tasked with taking it over the top, and the result is the motorcycle you see here. The FLHTCUSE reined as king of the full dressers, not just among Harley motorcycles but among all would-be mileage machines thanks to its huge compliment of equipment, unrivaled heritage, and unmistakable Harley-Davidson sound and feel. Simply put, "It's *the* high end dresser," said Jim Hofman, who directed the CVO branch when the FLHTCUSE was introduced.

When it was first offered in 2006, it had all the hallmarks of a great model right off the bat: the 103 cubic inch, fuel-injected, twin cam stroker motor and a bevy of Screamin' Eagle speed components guaranteed to achieve the passing and hauling power that touring bikes require. Hitting the magic number with factory stats of 100 foot-pounds of torque is just as important for bench racing as it is on the street. Rubber mounted in the frame and transmitting final drive via a Kevlar-reinforced belt, this fearsome mill brings power and pleasure to long haul-touring as well as taking it easy down the boulevards after a long day in the saddle.

For 2006 Harley-Davidson offered the Screamin' Eagle Ultra Classic Electra Glide motorcycle in three color combinations: Autumn Haze and Vivid Black (top), Black Candy Crimson and Charcoal Slate (middle), and Black Emerald and Majestic Green Pearl.

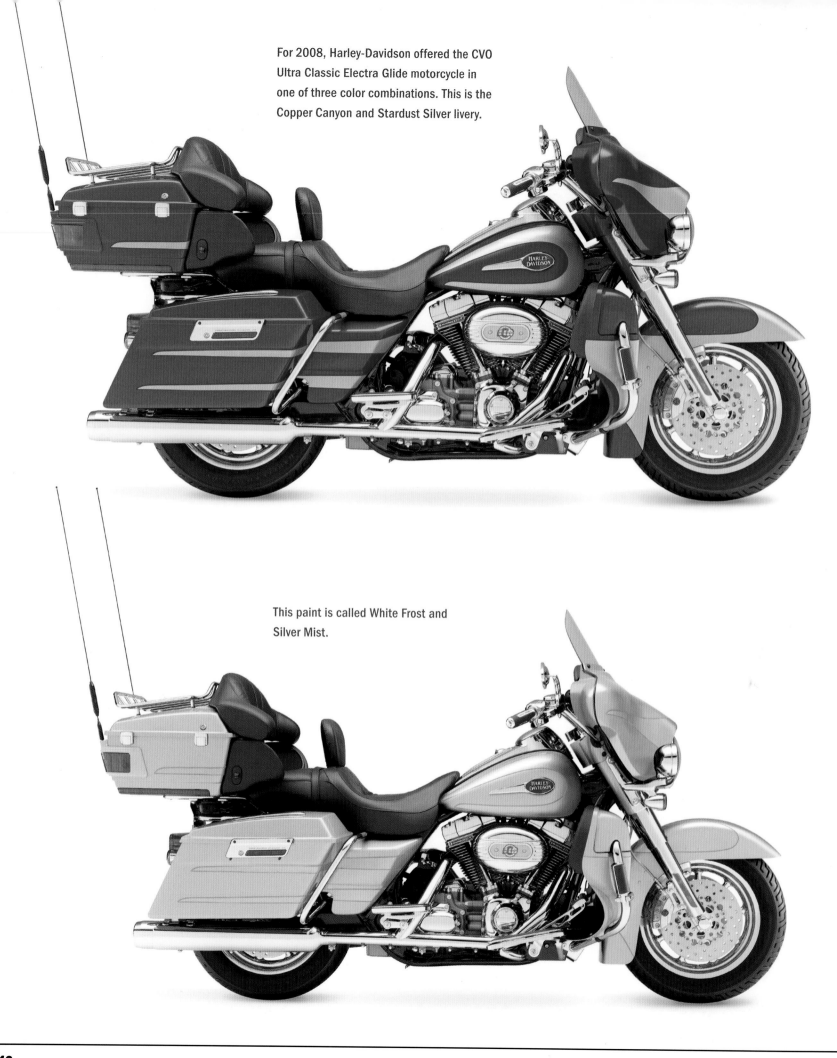

For 2008, Harley-Davidson offered the CVO Ultra Classic Electra Glide motorcycle in one of three color combinations. This is the Copper Canyon and Stardust Silver livery.

This paint is called White Frost and Silver Mist.

The third livery offered in 2008 was Crystal
Copper and Black Onyx.

BELOW:
Though the technology has changed dramati-
cally over the years, from above, the 2008
CVO Ultra Classic Electra Glide motorcycle retains the elemental V-twin riding
experience.

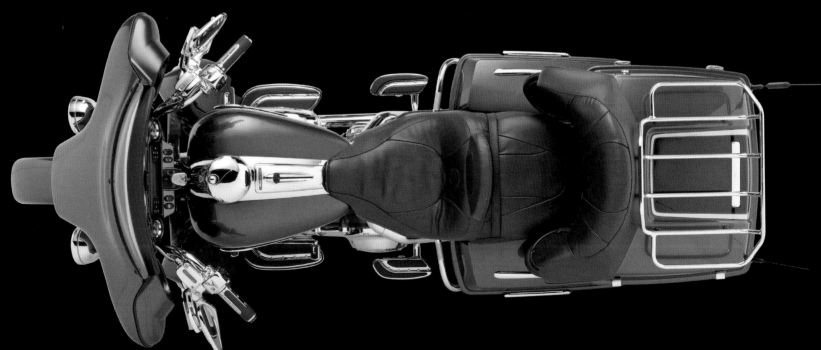

The 2008 CVO Ultra Classic Electra Glide
motorcycle was Harley-Davidson's ultimate
touring motorcycle with standard ABS brakes.

There's no shortage of touring gear, either. But "CVO" means going the extra mile, which results in distinctive touches and tweaks over the standard storage and convenience features. Take the Tour-Pak carrier, a standard item for long haul FL bikes: on the Screamin' Eagle Ultra Classic motorcycle, it's finished in custom leather for a head-turning look and luxurious feel. Same for the fairings: not only are the inner panels color-matched with exclusive paint, but the lowers get adjustable louvers for airflow control and the upper fairing is dressed up with more leather and spun aluminum gauge faces. A chopped and smoked windscreen perches up top, balancing function and form in the fine tradition of CVO motorcycle modifications.

Dig deeper and you'll find the luxury side of the equation cleverly hidden all around the motorcycle. A powerful Harman/Kardon stereo is tucked into the fairing with a pair of speakers, with more speakers in the passenger arm rests for more immersive sound, regardless of road speed and wind noise. And while the Stealth collection grips are handsome, the real treat is that they're heated, for cold mornings and windy nights. Ditto with the custom-stitched seats: heated front and rear, so warmth and comfort are never a problem.

As expected, a range of chrome accessories is available, as well as exclusive parts—from the air cleaner insert to the muffler caps and exclusive Screamin' Eagle timing and clutch covers. You can also chalk up the whole Stealth collection of grips, pegs and other bits. But, again, function is as important as flair. Just look at the

Combining this kind of range and comfort with this level of customization perfectly illustrates the Custom Vehicle Operation philosophy.

Autumn Haze and High Octane Orange 2009 CVO Ultra Classic Electra Glide motorcycles were the first CVO Electra Glide models to drop the "Screamin' Eagle" label.

dual-bulb headlamp for enhanced vision and visibility, the pushbutton gas cap and braided stainless steel brake and clutch lines that look sleek and hold up longer. Officially, "CVO" stands for "Custom Vehicle Operations," but when you feast your eyes on a machine like this, you can't help but wonder if the bike was put together according to MNC: "make no compromises"!

The first edition of the Screamin' Eagle Ultra Classic motorcycle came on the scene in 2006 with three paint schemes, ranging from the quiet and classy Black Candy Crimson and Charcoal Slate to the timeless Autumn Haze and Vivid Black; plus Black Emerald and Majestic Green Pearl, with enough contrast to turn heads for miles. By the time all three colors were in the hands of their new owners, the CVO motorcycle division knew they had a winner on their hands. So when the 2007 model came up to bat, they didn't have to change much . . . but they did.

"Resting on our laurels" isn't a phrase in the CVO vocabulary, and the 2007 edition of the Screamin' Eagle Ultra Classic motorcycle proved that point with a roar from its new 110 cubic inch twin cam motor, Harley's largest displacement motor yet. Bigger valves and ports, special pistons, and precision boring result in an exciting 115 foot-pounds to play with, giving you that much more headroom no matter what you're packing or where you're going. So the '07 is all that and a bag of chips in the engine room—but what's power without a way to get it to the rear wheel? Thankfully, the Ultra Classic motorcycle also received the six-speed Cruise Drive transmission to put all that power down, with more smoothness and efficiency but less noise and engine wear.

Cosmetically, the '07 Screamin' Eagle Ultra Classic motorcycle picked up a bevy of accessories, from the new Ironside collection, plus new 9-spoke aluminum wheels finished in chrome (of course). Color choices boiled down to Lightning Blue Pearl and Midnight Pearl; Black Ice and Electric Orange, and Light Candy Cherry and Black Ice—with Pearl accents on all colors. And there were functional upgrades, too, like new remote locks for the Tour-Pak carrier and saddlebags, plus the addition of an integrated navigation system in the fairing.

In 2010 Harley-Davidson used flame graphics to complement the Scarlet Red and Dark Slate paint on the CVO Ultra Classic Electra Glide motorcycle.

For 2014 Harley-Davidson offered the CVO Limited motorcycle in this Burgundy Blaze and Typhoon Maroon paint with Dragontail graphics.

The following year marked the first time a CVO model stayed on the books for more than two consecutive years. The '08 Screamin' Eagle Ultra Classic Electra Glide motorcycle definitely represented a break in "CVO" code at the time, but, then, giving the people what they want is more important than arbitrary rules!

What really ruled in '08 were the new electronic features that took the Screamin' Eagle Ultra Classic motorcycle to a new level of refinement and control. ABS brakes were now standard, producing controlled braking in less than optimum conditions. Placement of the ABS sensors do not interfere with the styling cues of the motorcycle.

This was also the year of taking some things away—like the throttle cable! While it ruffles the feathers of some Luddites, electronic throttle control simply delivers more precise fuel delivery in all conditions, for better tuning, fewer emission issues, and, most importantly . . . more power! Take it from Terry Roorda, editor of *Thunder Press*: "You get the most seamless, predictable, and gratifying performance manners of any Milwaukee machine to date."

Dain Gingerelli, reviewing the 2008 CVO models for *IronWorks*, agreed, saying: "The effortless push-pull for throttling up or down begins to spoil you. Indeed, you'll never look at a conventional throttle grip the same after experiencing the Ultra."

Other details shifted with the winds of change. The Tour-Pak carrier traded its handsome but heavier leather wrap for color-matched paint, while the tanks were upgraded to hold a whopping six gallons of fuel to stretch the road—and the rider's—endurance. But, as always, the miles melt away on a CVO machine, thanks to the carefully tuned suspension, and amenities. And when you reach your destination, you can admire one of the three exclusive color pairings: Copper and Stardust Silver; White Frost and Silver Mist; and the 105th Anniversary-exclusive, Crystal Copper and Black Onyx.

The next year brought a new name for a familiar face. In 2009, the Screamin' Eagle moniker was dropped—thankfully retaining the performance parts—and replaced with the simple CVO acronym. Thus, the 2009 CVO Ultra Classic Electra Glide motorcycle was reborn, with the same spirit of no-compromise luxury and touring but with a nominally shorter moniker. The real changes, though, were under the surface: not in the engine or the wiring, but in the frame itself.

The 2014 CVO Ultra Classic Electra Glide motorcycle featured a new two-piece cast frame.

Harley-Davidson called the color combination of the 2014 CVO Limited motorcycle Gold Rush and Carbon Dust.

In 2009 the CVO Ultra Classic Electra Glide motorcycle was the most luxurious touring model on the market.

Having soldiered on long enough, the single-piece tubular frame was replaced with a two-piece cast unit, a longer wheelbase, and more room for bigger tires. The rear was widened to accommodate a 180mm tire on a new 16-inch roulette-style wheel, while the front offered 130mm of tread on a 17-inch version of the roulette. More tire means more grip, and the new meats plus the frame upgrades received good reviews from all quarters of the motorcycling press.

Elsewhere, the new Rumble Collection of accessories debuted on the pegs, floor-boards, and grips, while the seat was modified inside and out for more double-takes and fewer rest-stop breaks. Greater storage and payload capacity resulted from a new Air-Wing rack on top of the Tour-Pak carrier and internal redesign of the saddlebags. And let's not forget about paint and graphics: Ruby Red and Typhoon Maroon; Autumn Haze and High Octane Orange; and Stardust Silver and Twilight Blue made the buying decision a challenge.

By now it was clear that the CVO Ultra Classic motorcycle wasn't just a flash in the pan, and it forged ahead from where the original Screamin' Eagle Electra Glide motorcycle started, picking up new features and upgrades every year like clockwork. The following year brought riders a host of upgrades, such as a new LED wraparound taillamp assembly built into the Tour-Pak carrier, plus a 12-volt accessory socket for charging the gizmos everyone had started to take for granted. The bags of the '10 model are illuminated for nighttime use with LED lamps, and include shaped liners to make unpacking a snap. Comfort-wise, the passenger is treated to a new adjustable backrest that lets you tweak the lumbar support to suit the choosiest of lower backs.

Colors for 2010 included Scarlet Red Pearl and Dark Slate; Riptide Blue and Titanium Dust; and Burnt Amber and Hot Citrus, all with flame graphics. But there was one more option that cranked up the exclusivity dial: a limited run of 999 motorcycles in Crimson Mist Black and Dark Slate with flame graphics. This model featured more than 100 different chrome and polished parts replaced with *black* finished pieces. The result is positively intimidating, a huge mass of cunning darkness menacing any street toward which it points its front wheel.

The next year, 2011, offered a quiet, some might say "stealthy," model, with pro-duction limited to just 1,500 in a single color: Black Ember and Rio Red with flame graphics. Technology upgrades show in the new Navigation Interface Module, linking the dash-mounted Road Tech Zumo 666 GPS unit to the radio speakers for easier operation. Diamond-cut inserts and badging grace the Tour-Pak carrier lid, CB pod, and SE Ventilator intake. The CVO motorcycle team even sent a shout-out to the passen-ger in the form of a new springboard-style suspension (integrated into the seat) and adjustable backrest, while looks and service were addressed with Contrast Chrome roulette wheels and Rumble Collection accessories from the Parts & Accessories Division. With so few of the 2011 CVO Ultra Classic Electra Glide motorcycles out there, it just might be a future classic. If you have one, keep it!

Attention to detail means that a CVO bagger looks good from any angle.

In 2014 the CVO Ultra Classic Electra Glide model was replaced by an even more exclusive model called, appropriately enough, the CVO Limited. Shown here is a 2015 example.

Harley-Davidson's Boom! Box audio system is one of the most powerful entertainment systems available.

In its seventh turn on the CVO motorcycle stage, the 2012 edition ramped up the entertainment quotient with a switch to a more powerful Boom! Audio System and established the tradition of including a CVO engraved iPod with CVO models. New Mirror Chrome Chisel wheels with matching rotors point the way, while handsome diamond-cut gauge faces make friends on lesser motorcycles green with envy. Plus, a new cylinder deactivation feature allowed for cooler engine temperatures while idling on a hot day. . . say, sitting in traffic at the Sturgis Rally. And continuing to dazzle without fail, paint and graphics artists produced three different paint schemes this year: Crystal Citron and Diamond Dust; Electric Orange and Black Diamond; and Wicked Sapphire and Stardust Silver, all enhanced with Big City Lights graphics.

The list of features for the CVO FLHTCUSE motorcycle had grown so extensive by now that it might take less time to say what the motorcycle *doesn't* have! (And that is no exaggeration.) As baggers reached unprecedented popularity, this motorcycle represented the "bagger of baggers," the cream of *any* crop, hands down. Riders of a CVO Ultra Classic Electra Glide motorcycle were assured of owning the most tricked-out, bedazzled machine ever to roll out of a factory anywhere around the globe.

The last call in 2013 was well timed: it was Harley-Davidson's 110th anniversary, a great sendoff for the longest-running CVO model to date, though this wasn't known at the time. CVO model designers and engineers were busy laying the groundwork for what came next—and they'd set themselves up with a helluva job, following an act like this.

LEFT:
From the very beginning, CVO motorcycles sported elegant custom touches like tinted fog lights.

OPPOSITE TOP:
Lighting it up with the CVO Ultra model.

OPPOSITE BOTTOM:
Natural beauty makes a great contrast for the carefully crafted beauty of the CVO Ultra Classic Electra Glide motorcycle.

In 2010 Harley-Davidson replaced over 100 chrome-plated pieces with black-finished pieces, giving the CVO Ultra Classic model a more menacing presence.

Upgrades included a switch to new Slipstream controls, tweaks to the audio for better integration and sound, plus a trio of new paint colors to round out the impressive pallet that the CVO Ultra Classic motorcycle had stacked up: Typhoon Maroon with Black Diamond and Burgundy Blaze; Stardust Silver with Dark Slate and Titanium Dust; and Tribal Orange with Dark Slate and Inferno Orange, all with Thunderblade graphics. But in this anniversary year, the Ultra Classic joined a host of carefully chosen 110th Anniversary special editions, giving buyers one more color option: the anniversary-exclusive Diamond Dust and Obsidian with Palladium graphics.

And with that, the CVO Ultra Classic Electra Glide motorcycle bowed to the upcoming Limited—only it didn't, not really. Like the Screamin' Eagle Electra Glide motorcycle, the CVO Ultra Classic motorcycle wasn't *replaced* so much as it was *reborn*. Like Harley-Davidson itself, this was a machine with staying power, and it would take more than a change in name to reshape the spirit of the longest running and most enduring CVO model, now or ever.

Contrast may turn heads, but it's the details that keep them looking.

ABOVE:
In 2012 Harley-Davidson offered the CVO Ultra Classic Electra Glide motorcycle in this stunning Crystal Citron and Diamond Dust livery.

In 2014 the CVO Ultra Classic motorcycle received a standard heated seat.

RIGHT:

The 2015 CVO Limited motorcycle came with the Motor Company's exceptional Daymaker LED Headlights and LED Fog Lamps as standard equipment.

BELOW:

Although stunning paint has been a part of the CVO motorcycle program from the very first FXR2 model, the Burnt Amber and Hot Citrus livery with flame graphics offered on the 2010 CVO Ultra Classic Electra Glide model was among the best of the best color combinations.

The command center on the CVO Ultra model has been upgraded with every model, but even from the earliest years it was comprehensive.

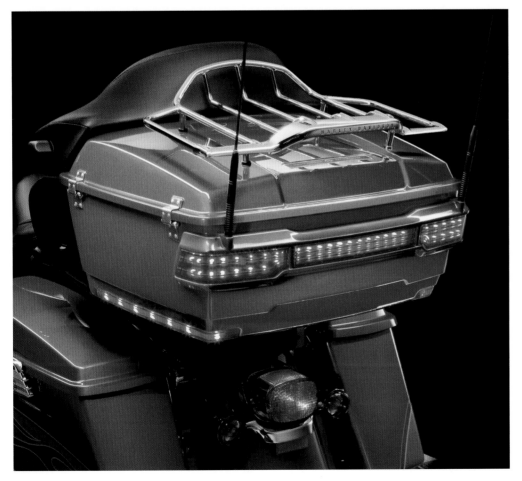

Leave it to CVO motorcycle group to take the classic Tour-Pak carrier and turn it up to eleven.

BELOW:
Owning a CVO Ultra model is the best seat in the house by far.

Nothing says Harley-Davidson like the two-tone Black Diamond and Inferno Orange livery offered on the 2011 CVO Street Glide motorcycle.

FLHXSE/ CVO STREET GLIDE AND CVO STREET GLIDE CUSTOM MODELS

If you want to know what kind of motorcycle is hot these days, just take a look around on a beautiful weekend in early spring or late fall. While some riders do most of their miles during their commutes and others save up for a big trip or two every year, *everyone* gets on the bike when the weekend hits and the sun is shining.

And when you're out on the road on that beautiful day, there's something that every motorcyclist notices: Street Glide motorcycles! Ridden by thousands of riders for as many reasons, it's become the very motorcycle that defines John Q. Public's mental picture when someone says "Harley-Davidson." From the beautifully proportioned and finished engine to the batwing fairing and unmistakable hard bags, the modern Street Glide motorcycle is Harley incarnate: a single street machine that is *the* motorcycle to any number of people. It's the mount of choice for fans of badass baggers, stereo-pounding street cruisers, the weekend tour set, even the custom builder's daily workhorse. In short, the Street Glide motorcycle has it all. That said, once the CVO branch gave it their magic touch, they put the FLHXSE CVO Street Glide motorcycle in a league of its own.

Contrast means class with a CVO paint job.

ABOVE:
No one does "custom" with the confidence and flair of the CVO motorcycle team.

OPPOSITE TOP:
A stiffer front fork made the 2015 CVO Street Glide model the best-handling touring motorcycle Harley Davidson had built to date.

The basic Street Glide motorcycle is already a solid machine, with an attitude and versatility that even more extravagantly appointed touring rigs can't quite match. So how do you pile on the enhancements of a CVO model that make a motorcycle like this so special, without making it more motorcycle than it needs to be? As anyone who's tried to drink a whole case of microbrew can tell you, too much of a good thing isn't always good!

But turning an already iconic and purposeful Harley-Davidson motorcycle into a CVO machine is more than an exercise in piling parts on the bike. The finished product has to be a coherent statement, a unified blend of art, power, and tradition. So instead of throwing the parts and accessories book at the CVO Street Glide motorcycle, the team took a more measured approach. To make the CVO Street Glide motorcycle a premium, exclusive Harley-Davidson motorcycle while keeping the stripped-down attitude and style that makes Street Glide motorcycles so popular and useful, they thought as much about what to take off as what to put on.

The basic layout of a batwing fairing—touring chassis, Big Twin powerplant, and a pair of hard bags—means the CVO motorcycle group started with solid raw material. The maiden CVO Street Glide motorcycle hit the scene in 2010, dialed up to 11 on the luxury and style scale while keeping a sleek profile and head-turning stance. As Harley-Davidson's premium entry into the custom bagger world, the bike had to be everything the rider wanted and needed, for both boulevard cruising and highway flying. It's easy to see how they struck that balance: beautifully!

In 2010 Harley-Davidson offered the CVO Street Glide motorcycle in this bold Candy Concord paint with Pale Gold Leaf graphics.

Let's take a look at the custom features that really make this motorcycle stand out when you pull up to the local poker run. First and foremost: the engine. Any custom worth its salt needs the power to back up the boasts made by the paint, chrome and other unique touches, and the CVO Street Glide motorcycle delivers. The Twin Cam 110 motor, exclusive to the CVO range in 2010, pumps out the kind of torque that gives asphalt nightmares: 113 foot-pounds, to be exact. It breathes in through a Screamin' Eagle air cleaner that proudly displays the displacement, so there's no doubt that you'll be checked out at stoplights. And that powerful rumble emits from a dual muffler exhaust, which brings the eye to another set of custom touches that make the CVO Street Glide motorcycle more than another cruiser with bags.

Check out that rear end: extended bags add visual length and a purposeful stance, while the rear fender blends in seamlessly with color-matched rear inserts, all integrated to frame the purposeful exhaust tips for a serious, muscle-bike-inspired look. Even smoother are the rear stop, tail, and turn lights built into handsome LED units with no protruding brackets or hardware to distract from the CVO Street Glide motorcycle's handsome lines. It's a set of custom touches that bolster the street-stalking profile of the machine with the factory quality and craftsmanship you only get from Harley-Davidson's CVO branch.

It's a good thing the rear end is so handsome, because, thanks to the bike's engine, your buddies will be seeing a lot of it. That powerful Twin Cam 110 sends its message to the road through the continually developed Cruise Drive six-speed transmission, which received a helical-cut fifth gear in 2010 for a quieter highway experience. And the *whoa* is right up there with the *go*, thanks to standard ABS and a trio of modern four-piston calipers clamping down on another trio of big 12-inch rotors.

But it wouldn't be any good to turn such a fundamentally versatile motorcycle into just another stoplight hero, so the CVO motorcycle team dove into the suspension to keep the experience premium. The key was to give the bike that slammed custom bagger stance that everyone loves while handling well, staying comfortable, and doing it all with luggage and a passenger: no easy task. CVO motorcycle engineers strategically separated the compression and rebound damping duties between the two rear shocks, with compression duties in the right hand shock and rebound in the left. A technique used in the front forks of racing motorcycles, the result is excellent rear-end control and comfortable compliance. According to Steve Natt, writing for *Cycle World*, this engineering results in a motorcycle that's "darn near flickable . . . light on corner entry and easy to pick up with the throttle on the exit." High praise for a slammed custom bagger!

Even the versatile Street Glide motorcycle gets a host of luxuries and conveniences.

ABOVE:
Bold contrast and aggressive graphics made the 2015 CVO Street Glide model one of the boldest CVO motorcycles yet.

LEFT:
Hard candy metal flake and CVO motorcycles are a match made in heaven.

TOP:
Nobody nails custom bagger touches like the CVO motorcycle group.

ABOVE RIGHT:
There's no shortage of acreage on a CVO touring machine for custom paint and striping.

ABOVE:
Even though it was no longer its official title, Harley-Davidson paid homage to the past by giving the 2010 CVO Street Glide motorcycle "Screamin' Eagle" tank graphics.

That slammed look goes even further with some serious rolling stock, and this machine is no exception. The seven-spoke Agitator wheels are a serious 18-inch-tall front and rear, a perfect balance between an eye-grabbing front end and one that still turns like a well-tuned factory bike (I'm looking at *you*, 30-inch wheels!). They're finished in a handsome contrast chrome finish, adding a mean edge to this classic machine. Even the front fender gets reshaped and trimmed to show off the rolling stock. Other handsome details include custom Rumble Collection grips, pegs, and floorboard inserts, plus custom French stitching on the saddle and backrest.

But nothing's more classic than a Harley-Davidson motorcycle with a killer paint job, and lucky owners of 2010 CVO Street Glide motorcycles had three delicious colors to choose from: Candy Concord, Spiced Rum, and Tequila Sunrise, all with Pale Gold Leaf graphics that are, of course, real gold. How much more bling can you get?

The 2010 iteration of the CVO Street Glide motorcycle was such a hit that it stayed on for 2011, with only minor changes. Those with a sharp memory can split the two model years by the paint schemes, which are even more exclusive than the CVO machines themselves. For 2011, CVO Street Glide motorcycles were available in four distinct color combinations: Autumn Haze and Antique Gunstock; Black Diamond and Inferno Orange; Kryptonite and Black Diamond; and Black Diamond with Crimson Tag graphics.

Harley-Davidson offered the 2010 CVO Street Glide motorcycle in this Spiced Rum paint with Gold Leaf graphics.

Although the 2010 CVO Street Glide motorcycle looked like a cut-down custom, it had everything a rider could need for long-haul touring.

For 2012's CVO Street Glide motorcycle, the big news was heard more than seen: a Harman Kardon stereo with two amps pumping 400 watts into eight speakers. Read that line again, twice if you have to, and you'll have to admit that these numbers represent a seriously earth-shaking sound system! The 2012 CVO Street Glide motorcycle has one of its amps stashed in the fairing with four of the speakers, a pair of speakers in the fairing lowers, two more in the saddlebag lids, and the last amp in the saddlebag. There would have been more speakers and amps in the attic, but the CVO motorcycle group kept that accessory off the option list!

There were new paint schemes this time around too: Ruby Red and Typhoon Maroon; Hot Citrus and Antique Gunstock; and Dark Slate and Black Diamond, all with alluring Phantom Flame graphics. Other upgrades for the 2012 edition included a chrome-finished 19-inch front wheel, plus an upgraded touring seat with removable passenger backrest.

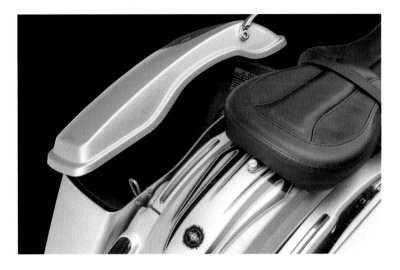

ABOVE:

One-touch latches mean easier loading and unloading, no matter the situation.

BELOW:

Ultra graphics, ultra power.

The Splitstream vent was developed in the wind tunnel and on the road for maximum comfort.

The paint on the 2011 CVO Street Glide motorcycle is so astonishing that it attracts as much attention as any scenery in which it finds itself parked.

BELOW:
Because the CVO Street Glide motorcycle didn't have a trunk, Harley-Davidson's CVO motorcycle team mounted the rear speakers in the saddlebags.

The command center on the latest CVO models makes the cockpit of the space shuttle look antiquated.

As favored as the CVO Street Glide motorcycle was, part of the factory custom mission is to add fresh inspiration on a regular basis, so the model was rotated out after 2012. But that only lasted until 2015, when Harley-Davidson's comprehensive Project Rushmore upgrades brought even more refinement to the Street Glide motorcycle. The most iconoclastic feature is the new Twin-Cooled Twin Cam 110 engine, and no matter what you think about mixing oil and water, more power is always better. But it's not all about the motor, of course. From the wind-tunnel-tested fairing to the keyless ignition system, plus serious lighting and braking upgrades, Project Rushmore brought a host of details that add up to more than the sum of their parts.

On the styling front, the CVO Street Glide motorcycle gets some help in the form of a set of polished chrome Aggressor wheels, 19 inches in the front and 18 inches in the back. And while handsome wheels will always turn heads, there's something new lurking under the skin: a stereo that puts almost everything on the road to shame, no matter how many wheels we're talking about. The 2015 CVO Street Glide motorcycle packs an all new Boom! Audio System, boasting a total of 600 watts of power from a pair of amplifiers, all integrated into the 6.5-inch touch display in the fairing. Who said luxury cars are the only places you'll find sophisticated infotainment systems like this?

There are new colors, of course, featuring some options on both ends of the show-stopper scale. On the subtle-but-beautiful end, you have Carbon Crystal with Phantom Flames as well as Starfire Black with Gold Dust Flames, both whispering "luxury" while letting craftsmanship speak for itself. But if you want them to see your CVO motorcycle coming a mile away, check out Ultraviolet Blue with Molten Lava Flames, and the eye-watering metal flakes in the Hard Candy Mercury with Smokey Quartz Flames.

These updates really bring the FLHXSE into the forefront of the CVO lineup, a shining example of how much motorcycle you can pack into such a versatile chassis while maintaining the stripped, slammed profile this model is known for. As an exercise in attitude, it requires no explanation. But as a motorcycle, it glides to the front of the pack: the king of the baggers, proudly rolling past all others on the way to adventure.

Integrated turn and brake lamps use LEDs for maximum visibility and style.

We're so accustomed to touch screens, the CVO motorcycle team thought we might as well feel at home on our ride too.

Phantom Flame graphics adorn the Hot Citrus and Antique Gunstock paint on this 2012 CVO Street Glide motorcycle.

Harley-Davidson offered the CVO Street Glide
motorcycle for the first time in 2010.

FLTRUSE CVO ROAD GLIDE ULTRA MOTORCYCLE

Batwings. On any given Sunday, weather permitting, you can see them swarming on highways and backroads all over America. And why not? Harley-Davidson's batwing fairing is a symbol of American motorcycling, and one of the telltale ways to identify a Harley coming down the highway from a distance. For newer enthusiasts just getting into the sport, it's natural to gravitate toward the things you (and others!) recognize. Hence the fleets of Electra Glide, Ultra Classic, and Street Glide motorcycles you can find out and about when the weather is kind and the ride is easy.

But there's another option, lurking deep and quietly in Harley-Davidson's moto-offerings both past and current. Put simply: the Road Glide motorcycle. Even though its ancestors hail from the same decade that brought us the Super Glide, bell-bottoms, and the Average White Band, there are those who contend that it's just not a "traditional" Harley motorcycle. But that's nitpicking. Enlightened riders like Terry Roorda of *Thunder Press* know that the CVO Road Glide Ultra motorcycle "owes more conceptually to the Tour Glide Ultra Classic of the '90's than to any predecessor in its Road Glide lineage." Tradition runs deep in this one, with its long-lauded, frame-mounted fairing, so it's time to knock the naysayers back on their heels: the CVO Road Glide Ultra motorcycle, the most evolved example of the breed, does everything

The Screamin' Eagle Road Glide model in its natural habitat: the road!

In 2009 Harley-Davidson offered the CVO Road Glide motorcycle in Electric Orange and Vivid Black, a variation on the Motor Company's corporate colors.

OPPOSITE TOP:

Bill Davidson introduces the 2009 CVO Road Glide motorcycle.

OPPOSITE BOTTOM:

Scott Miller rolls out on the new FLTRUSE at the 2010 Summer Dealer Meeting.

a "traditional" Harley motorcycle is expected to do. Specifically, to put down the miles commandingly, look like a million bucks, and kick ass from Yuma to Yonkers, no matter what the road throws down.

From the tall, reduced-angle windscreen to the distinctive sharknose fairing, new wind deflectors, and spacious Tour-Pak carrier, it's clear that the CVO branch churned out this go-anywhere, do-anything machine for the road warriors and long-haul heroes of the highway. Sunday drivers need not apply—this sumptuous rig is carefully tailored for melting the miles away.

Start with the full complement of touring accessories, all enhanced with thoughtful and handsome CVO adornments from top to bottom. Sure, there's a Tour-Pak carrier, but this one features handsome LED taillights, plus a 12-volt power socket on the inside along with interior lighting, so there's no fumbling in the dark when Mother Nature sends you searching for your rain gear. Plus, it's topped with an Air Wing luggage rack. Two-up riding always requires more space, right?

Speaking of space, the traditional hard bags are shaped to take more than a weekend's worth of goods and goodies, but the Road Glide Ultra motorcycle's special treatment includes luggage liners for fast and easy unpacking. And those bags lock at a touch of the key fob, along with the Tour-Pak carrier and the ignition, for peace of mind no matter where the road takes you. Plus, an iPod Nano is included with the bike, stashed in the saddlebag to link up to the stereo and keep a full charge. If all this sounds like more than a motorcycle needs, maybe you just haven't yet enjoyed the pleasures of total touring Harley-Davidson-style.

The 2000 Screamin' Eagle Road Glide motorcycle was the first non-FXR model that the CVO motorcycle team produced.

More good news: the CVO Road Glide Ultra motorcycle affords both the rider and passenger plenty of long-haul comfort, thanks to one of the most sumptuous seats in the industry. More than just a piece of foam, the passenger and rider perches are both internally suspended, keeping the roughest roads and longest miles from wearing out your precious parts. But there's more: these thrones are tricked out to the max, with adjustable front and rear backrests, plus electric seat heaters and even a four-way lumbar support for the back seat. It's not always bad being the passenger with treats like these.

Not that the rider gets the short end of the stick on the CVO Road Glide Ultra motorcycle. To the contrary, the cockpit is as fully featured and well-thought-out as anything on two wheels —or four! Spacious floorboards keep you mobile and comfy as the states fly by, while the handlebars have been tweaked for long-distance comfort and internally wired for a clean, custom look. Cruise control is present for easy speed control when the road opens up, while a Harman Kardon amp drives four Boom! speakers to push back the wind and fill the miles with your favorite tunes. Plus, the stereo is set up for the whole nine, like an intercom system and XM radio. If it sounds like a lot for your standard rotor and stator team to handle, don't worry! Harley engineers have configured an updated charging system to handle the extra work.

Sure, that's a lot of comfort and utility, but how does it get down the road? Thanks to a Screamin' Eagle Twin Cam 110, the Road Glide Ultra motorcycle is locked and loaded for everything from top-gear roll-ons to first-gear tire smoking, thanks to enough cubic inches to belt out more than 100 foot-pounds of torque. But a CVO motorcycle has to be as refined as it is powerful, so the engine tuning and fueling are carefully tweaked. "Throttle response is impeccable," said Kevin Duke of *motorcycle.*

ABOVE:
In addition to Electric Orange and Vivid Black, Harley-Davidson offered the 2000 Screamin' Eagle Road Glide motorcycle in this pretty three-tone red livery.

BELOW:
Harley brought the Screamin' Eagle Road Glide motorcycle back for the 2001 model year.

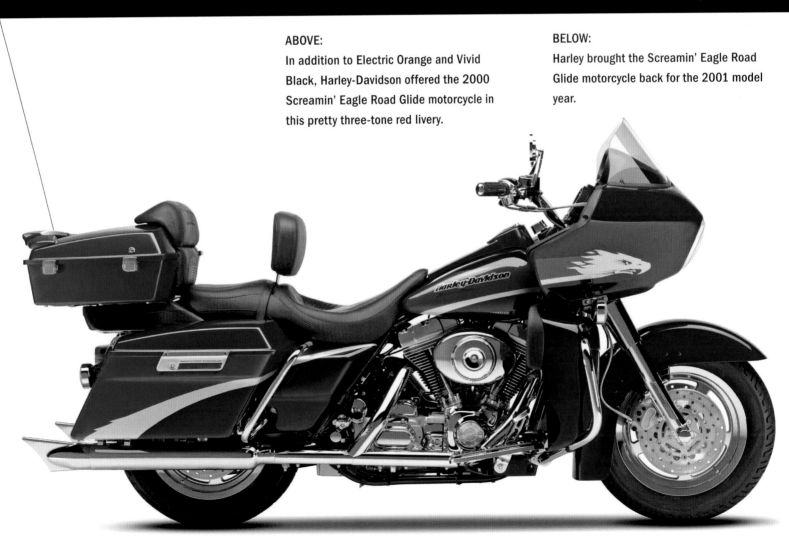

The 2002 Screamin' Eagle Road Glide motorcycle was little changed from the popular 2000 and 2001 versions. As the years progressed, each model year would see an increase in customization.

com, "with ultra-smooth pickup from a closed throttle." Tractable, plus enough power to pull a full load briskly and more, but it's also got the legs to get you to the horizon. With a full six gallons in the tank, the Road Glide Ultra motorcycle can stretch its legs for more than 250 miles on a stint. And there's plenty of braking power to slow you down when things get rough, thanks to a trio of Brembo four-piston calipers backed up by ABS braking. Because all the power in the world won't get you home without the control to manage it.

Not that you'll want to go home with this much motorcycle to show off. As you're bound to know by now, no CVO machine rolls off the line without enough detail work and custom touches to sweep your local bike show without breaking a sweat. And while all of the rolling art from the CVO motorcycle department gets way *more* than your average Harley-Davidson, bikes like the Road Glide Ultra motorcycle get even *more* on top of that. Just look at it: there's more room for sumptuous paint and graphics, more room for speakers and other electronics, just more motorcycle from top to bottom. All that acreage makes a prime canvas for the trademark CVO motorcycle paint treatment, which hit the scene in 2011 with three bold color combinations for lucky owners to choose from: subtle Charcoal Slate with Black Twilight; classic Frosted Ivory with Vintage Gold; and the striking Rio Red with Black Ember, all highlighted with Quartzite Graphics. Other details include a big scoop of accessories from the Rumble Collection for the controls, latches, and other areas, all highlighted with the rich chrome for which Harley-Davidson motorcycles are rightly famous.

But the real shine is on the rolling stock, via an unmistakable pair of 18-inch Agitator wheels, finished in mirror chrome and sporting a sharp look that will turn heads from one state line to the next.

After a multi-year hiatus, the Road Glide Ultra motorcycle was back for more in 2015, a big boon to the discerning riders who missed out on the first round in 2011. Along with CVO motorcycle's typical high-caliber treatment, the 2015 CVO Road Glide Ultra model also gets pumped up from a host of Harley-Davidson's Project Rushmore enhancements. Improvements include the Reflex linked ABS braking system, further refinements to the sharknose fairing's aerodynamic performance (thanks to triple splitstream vents), and ergonomic touches top to bottom that sharpen and improve every mile of the riding experience. It might be called the FLTRUSE, but the 2015 CVO Road Glide Ultra motorcycle still packs tons of enhancements that always appealed to the road-focused rider—including the new Twin-Cooled Twin Cam 110 engine, a combination of air-cooled and precision liquid-cooling methods—for peak performance in more road environments than ever. Curb-spotters can pick out the 2015 version by its Chrome Slicer wheels, or by one of the three color combinations available: Abyss Blue with Crushed Sapphire; Burgundy Blaze with Typhoon Maroon; or Carbon Dust with Autumn Sunset. And if that doesn't work, you'll be able to hear the upgraded Boom! Box Infotainment System from miles away! Of course, one glance at that singular fairing wrapping dual headlights ought to do it, too.

In 2009, after a seven-year hiatus, the Road Glide model returned to the CVO motorcycle lineup.

For riders looking for a frame-mounted fairing fitted to their ultimate touring motorcycle, Harley-Davidson offered the 2015 CVO Road Glide Ultra motorcycle.

ABOVE:
Harley-Davidson called this color combination Carbon Dust and Sunset Autumn.

RIGHT:
The 2015 CVO Road Glide Ultra motorcycle featured an innovative combined rear stop-turn-taillight unit.

But no matter what year or color combo strikes your fancy, the CVO Road Glide Ultra motorcycle is the absolute king of the long road, a model whose roots run deeper than most know. It's the mount of choice for those in the know, riders who don't need a batwing fairing to confirm they're riding a Harley-Davidson motorcycle, through and through.

The 2015 CVO Road Glide Ultra motorcycle offered an inner fairing that was color matched to the body paint.

FLTRXSE ROAD GLIDE CUSTOM MOTORCYCLE

Since the Shovelhead-powered Tour Glide motorcycle broke onto the scene at the dawn of the 1980s, Harley-Davidson Touring riders have been stuck with a tough decision that starts with a simple question: sharknose or batwing? While some may raise their eyebrows at this strange animal talk, the Harley-Davidson faithful nod solemnly when they hear these terms compared. The fairing is literally the face of a Harley Touring rig, and every rider wants to put their best face forward when they're out on the open road.

Hence the classic dilemma. Riders tend toward one camp or the other, though the classic FL and the Road Glide models are *both* handsome, purposeful machines. But no matter which way you lean, there's no denying that the CVO Road Glide Custom motorcycle of 2012 and 2013 is a helluva nice machine. Even the batwing faithful have to admire its sleek profile, muscular stance, and numerous custom details. After all, this isn't just any touring bike: it's a CVO machine.

Some riders prefer the frame-mounted fairing of the Road Glide motorcycle series because it doesn't feed wind input into the front wheel. Others just think it looks great.

All the same, a touring bike without a fairing is just a motorcycle, but the Road Glide Custom fairing is more than just a handsome face. Rigidly mounted to the frame of the motorcycle, it doesn't pull at the handlebars or affect the steering when crosswinds or wind blasts make their presence known. It's even topped with an aerodynamically tuned Wind Splitter screen, smoked for a sinister look. Like the original Tour Glide motorcycle, it packs two headlamps instead of one, but the Road Glide Custom motorcycle ups the ante thanks to its powerful twin Daymaker lamps. More light is always helpful when it comes to seeing more and being seen.

Speaking of being seen, the Road Glide Custom motorcycle is a great machine for turning heads. When it broke onto the scene in 2012, three color combinations were available to the envy of lesser makes and models: White Gold Pearl with Starfire Black; Maple Metallic with Vivid Black; and Candy Cobalt with Twilight Blue, all backed up by alluring Real Smoke graphics. It wears any of these colors well, with the pairings smoothed sensually from the fairing onto the tank, and from the side covers onto the saddlebags for a sleek, cohesive look. Get closer and you'll notice more, like the Rumble Collection details throughout the bike. Functional black rubber meets handsome chrome on the floorboard inserts, footpegs, pedals, and grips, balancing the flash-and-malice combination that gives the Road Glide Custom motorcycle its presence, on the road or at the curb.

But no matter where you roll on this tricked-out CVO motorcycle, one thing is certain: they'll hear you coming. The bassline comes courtesy of a Screamin' Eagle tuned Twin Cam 110 powerplant, with modern engine control features like an electronic throttle and electronically metered Sequential Port Fuel Injection to get every ounce of power from that big engine. Rubber mounted in the frame for all-day comfort and vibration damping, it's also rated for 122 foot-pounds of torque. Plus there's the aptly named Heavy Breather air intake, finished in black with bright aluminum details, wrapping the filter element for a look that says "performance" all the way to town. Out back, the dual-chrome exhaust features chrome and black endcaps on twin four-inch mufflers for a thrumming tone you'll want to listen to all the way to the horizon. Fed through a tough-as-nails Cruise Drive six-speed, this high-powered prescription is just what the doctor ordered, whether you're launching from a stoplight or are on a two-up weekend jaunt.

In addition to looking wicked cool, the LED headlights light up the road like the sun itself.

Meanwhile, the rest of the symphony streams from a 200-watt twin-channel Harman Kardon Audio System, pumping through an array of MTX audio speakers and tweeters to round out the highs. And since CVO models get all the trimmings, this bike comes with an iPod garnished with custom Bar and Shield engraving, ready to rock. The result is a powerful system that gets the job done at any speed. In a comparison between the 2013 CVO Road Glide Custom motorcycle and a Honda Goldwing F6B, Don Canet of *Cycle World* wrote ". . . enjoyed rocking the miles away, the Harley's four woofers and six tweeters letting me hear the tunes above the wind noise and the thrum of the big V-twin, even at highway speeds." Because when the CVO motorcycle team puts a stereo on a bike, it's not going to be just *any* stereo: it's going to be worthy of the CVO name.

All that powerful sound wouldn't go anywhere without a set of badass wheels, and the CVO Road Glide Custom motorcycle isn't left wanting. Show-stopping Agitator wheels are cast from aluminum and finished in a unique Contrast Chrome finish, sized to turn heads with a 19-inch up front and an 18-inch in the rear. The looks are backed up by custom Agitator brake rotors, the twin-disc floating front setup tweaked to provide all the stopping power this beast needs when the go needs some whoa. But this is a machine built for the road, not just the bike show scene, so ABS braking is included to maintain control during braking events, no matter what the road throws at you.

Harley-Davidson offered the 2013 CVO Road Glide Custom motorcycle in this Roman Gold and Burnt Emerald color combination with Edge graphics.

The comfort level of the 2015 CVO Road Glide Ultra motorcycle was so high that stopping to admire the scenery was optional.

Not that the CVO Road Glide Custom motorcycle can't turn heads without turning a wheel. A custom bagger all the way, it invites stares and questions no matter where it's parked. And that's all down to the extra effort put in behind the scenes: routing all the hand-control wiring inside the bars, extending the hard bags to blend seamlessly with a color-matched rear fascia, even LED lamps for extra brightness and a sharp, custom look. What's more, the seat is treated with a unique, quilted design highlighted by color-matched stitching and a removable passenger pillion so you can show off your swagger with someone special or roll solo.

The CVO Road Glide Custom motorcycle stayed in the lineup in 2013, when it was enhanced with an even more exclusive treatment than CVO models already receive. The limited-production 110th Anniversary Edition CVO Road Glide Custom motorcycle was dolled up in an exclusive Diamond Dust and Obsidian paint scheme with Palladium graphics that included special gas tank medallions and a serialized plaque to commemorate 110 years of two-wheeled excellence. These rare beasts also featured a custom finish on the powertrain components and further anniversary touches on the seat. What better way to celebrate the occasion than a fierce motorcycle like this?

BELOW:
A 2011 CVO Road Glide Ultra model with the warm tones of familiar wood and leather.

OPPOSITE BOTTOM:
CVO adornments sharpen the already aggressive profile of the Road Glide.

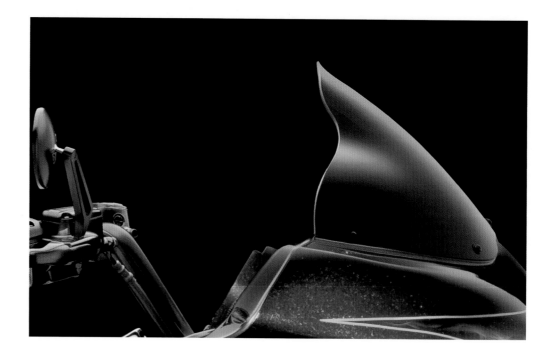

RIGHT:
Wind tunnel testing mates style with performance.

OPPOSITE:
If you want to see the world, there's no mount like a CVO touring machine.

BELOW:
In 2011 the GPS unit mounted to the handlebars of the CVO Road Glide Ultra motorcycle.

This 2011 CVO Road Glide Ultra model wears Charcoal Slate and Black Twilight livery with Quartzite graphics.

This 2012 CVO Road Glide motorcycle in Candy Cobalt and Twilight Blue paint highlighted by Real Smoke graphics features a Screamin' Eagle Heavy Breather air filter cover.

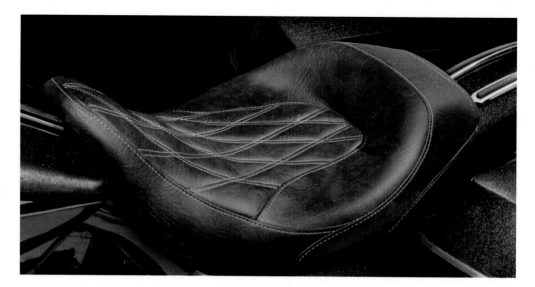

ABOVE:

Although the seat on a touring motorcycle is designed for comfort first and foremost, on a CVO Road Glide motorcycle it is also designed to look as great as the rest of the machine.

TOP:

The artistic customized touches on the 2012 CVO Road Glide Ultra motorcycle qualify the machine as rolling sculpture.

ABOVE MIDDLE:

The quality of the sound systems used on CVO motorcycles would be unimaginable to riders a generation ago.

ABOVE BOTTOM:

Infotainment moved to a whole new level for 2015.

RIGHT:

You *can* take it with you, and in style.

But even the normal CVO Road Glide Custom motorcycle (as if any CVO motorcycle could be "normal") received further tweaks for the 2013 model year. The hand and foot controls received parts from Harley-Davidson's Slipstream Collection, while new LED headlamp units lit the way and gave the front of the bike an even meaner look. Two other non-anniversary color combinations were available, too: Roman Gold with Burnt Emerald, and Atomic Orange with Galaxy Grey, both highlighted with Edge graphics.

What it all comes down to is attitude. From the custom paintwork to the cohesive detailing, blacked-out components balance perfectly with chrome highlights and that sharknose fairing points the way. The CVO Road Glide Custom motorcycle is one bad bagger with the soul of a shark. The 2001 and 2002 CVO Road Glide motorcycles (with the screamin' eagle graphics) were iconic, and were the first CVO motorcycles to feature increased engine displacement (a hallmark throughout the short history of CVO motorcycles). They also helped put CVO models as well as the Road Glide motorcycle on the map.

ABOVE:

The optional White Gold Pearl and Starfire Black livery on the 2012 CVO Road Glide Custom motorcycle took contrast to a whole new level.

BELOW:

Even earth tones complement the custom paintwork on many CVO models.

Caught in the wild: the 2011 FLTRU in the beautiful nation of Brazil.

CHAPTER 3

Bill Davidson introduces the CVO Fat Bob motorcycle at the 2008 Summer Dealer Meeting.

DYNA MOTORCYCLES:
SLEEK
CVO MODELS

SCREAMIN' EAGLE FXDWG^2 & SCREAMIN' EAGLE FXDWG^3 MODELS

When Harley-Davidson released the 2001 Screamin' Eagle FXDWG^2 motorcycle, the custom vehicle division was still quite young. This was just the third year and the fifth vehicle in the program after the original three FXR motorcycles and two Road Glide motorcycles in 1999 and 2000. Looking back now, with so many wildly popular CVO touring models on the roster, a factory-custom Dyna motorcycle might seem like a departure from the mission. But when you put it in context, the focus is all there.

Like any piece of fine art, CVO machines benefit from the human touch.

The first Dyna-framed, factory-built motorcycles debuted in 1991 with the release of the limited edition FXDB Sturgis model, a factory custom before there was a term for factory customs. At the time, the Dyna motorcycle was viewed by some as the successor to the FXR model, but you could say that the Dyna motorcycle's roots go back in H-D lore further still, even to the early 1970s.

As H-D's first production motorcycle to blend a Big Twin chassis and engine with a smaller, leaner Sportster model front end, the 1971 Super Glide model was a production motorcycle that mimicked contemporary custom trends. From a manufacturing point of view, it might seem like a radical response to what independent chop shops

were doing, but it was actually a rational reaction for a company that has always watched the custom scene for current trends.

As custom choppers maintained popularity, H-D's factory chopper theme continued with the slammed and raked FX Low Rider model in 1977, then the Fat Bob model in 1979. The FX Wide Glide motorcycle pushed the envelope even further when it took the stage in 1980 with wider triple clamps, longer forks, and a tall thin 21-inch front wheel. Yes, Harley-Davidson was wisely picking up on the styling cues and handling traits that riders wanted and leveraging factory production techniques to deliver motorcycles of style and performance. In terms of looks, the common element binding these models is the influence of Willie G. Davidson, a connection worth noting.

So when the Dyna line debuted with the Sturgis model in 1991, its potent presence revealed familiar DNA, even though the new Dyna chassis was substantially evolved from prior FL and FXR platforms. As it happened, the one-year-only Sturgis model became the springboard for a series of Dyna models that included the Dyna Low Rider and the Dyna Wide Glide models in 1993—and even the Dyna Super Glide model in 1995—bringing us full circle.

It was déjà vu all over again in 2001 when the Dyna Wide Glide motorcycle joined the still-young factory custom program, identified as FXDWG[2]. Product planners and engineers made the most of the still-raked wide front end, bobbed fenders, traditional coil-over suspension, forward controls, and 21-inch front wheel. So why *not* tap into the Dyna motorcycle's lengthy heritage? It's something to be proud of and also something to celebrate.

In fact, there are those who say the WG in this model name isn't a mere designation of the bike's front end, but actually in honor of Willie G. It's an exquisite motorcycle, strutting out in Scarlet Red with hand-applied 23-karat gold leaf flames. The

With the demise of the FXR platform, Harley-Davidson's CVO motorcycle team turned to the Dyna chassis.

The Dyna Wide Glide model made an ideal platform for creating a bespoke CVO motorcycle custom.

headline on a brochure published at the time claimed, "Cars have to be upside down and on fire to get this much attention"—and that was the truth. The Dyna model was a traffic stopper then, as it is today. It took to the highway faster than any other model in the lineup, too; everyone knows the speed-enhancing properties of red paint, right?

But let's take a closer look at those gold leaf flames on the fairing, tank, and fender. It's difficult to tell in a photograph, but up close and in-person you can see slight variations in the gold leaf application, some light edges and seams. According to Jim Hofman, they felt that it looked "unfinished." When they brought this up to Ray Drea, H-D's chief stylist and the man in charge of paint and graphics, his response was, "That's because it's true gold leaf and that's how gold leaf looks. It's up to you guys to explain it to the press and the customers."

Drea was right on. Actual gold leaf application, such as on bank windows and fire engines back in the day, consists of creating a design, placing the glue, then pressing the leaf into the glue. It's a one-at-a-time hand operation that shows variations; no two lines will be identical. Said Hofman, "Ray was not going to use a decal or sticker, he wanted true gold leaf. He wanted these to be genuine pieces of art." And that's what they are. Such close attention to authenticity and precision execution have been elements in the production of CVO motorcycles from the beginning, and this incident stands out as one striking example.

In the engine department, the CVO Dyna motorcycle runs an 88 cubic inch Silver and Chrome Twin Cam engine. All Dyna motorcycle engines are rubber mounted, too, reducing engine vibration on this lightest, best handling of the Big Twins. Like production Dyna motorcycles, this one has a slim front fender and wider triple trees netting a beefier look. Chrome bits are everywhere, from the bars and hand controls to the fuel tank console with its silver-faced speedometer and oval air cleaner. Color-matched components include the frame, headlight nacelle, chin spoiler, coil cover, battery box, tank, and fenders. The tan leather seat is genius, style-wise, incorporating genuine ostrich inserts. Lightningstar wheels, a 21-inch up front—of course—and a 16-inch on the back blend with lowered suspension at both ends for a street-hugging stance; even standing still it's a hot-rod motorcycle coiled and ready to leap. With so few built, this model was destined from birth to become a future classic among cruisers.

The 2001 factory custom version of the Dyna Wide Glide motorcycle had been so well received that, when the next model year rolled around, there was little need to make changes, other than adding a number "3" to the end of the model name: FXDWG³. Of course, the paint schemes always had to change each year; that was gospel in this department. When you change the paint and graphics, you have a different model, even if little else has been altered, ensuring that owners have the very latest factory custom off the line. The CVO model's intricate and multi-layered paint schemes always speak to customer appeal and model distinction.

The FXDWG³ model was offered in Navy Blue Pearl with Silver Metallic Flames; and Vivid Black with Gold Flames. It sported the same 1450cc Twin Cam engine with Silver & Chrome finish.

Harley-Davidson Dyna models were regarded as the road-ready performance customs of the line at the turn of the millennium. Their longtime popularity over many years continues to bear out this solid character, which encourages the rider to flick the throttle and go. Maybe that's why the factory custom development team nicknamed the CVO Dyna Wide Glide project "Switchblade," one of the few times an internal moniker has leaked to the public and stuck.

The CVO Wide Glide motorcycle is all about dramatic lines and contrast.

When you take a model with all the right historic cues and crank up its appeal, with limited edition paint and extra chrome, then build only a very small number of them, you have the precise recipe for an instant icon. That's the story of the FXDWG[2] and FXDWG[3] models: motorcycles of distinction in their time that have become even more coveted today.

At home on Capital Drive.

FXDSE SCREAMIN' EAGLE DYNA LOW RIDER MODEL

Only once before, for two consecutive model years in 2001 and 2002, did Dyna models take to the stage in factory custom attire. Those were the FXDWG[2] and FXDWG[3] models. If that exercise was about recognizing the Dyna motorcycle's place in H-D model history, then, in model year 2007, it was about securing the Dyna motorcycle's vitality for the future.

As the decade progressed, H-D engineers had been paying the Dyna platform more attention. The 2006 production Dyna motorcycles had received beefier 49mm forks, a newly designed chassis, and the six-speed Cruise Drive transmission. The Cruise Drive transmission was highly praised for features such as an improved shifting mechanism, helical-cut gears, and the lighter clutch effort it afforded. For a model like the Dyna motorcycle, with its superior power-to-weight ratio, these qualities only enhanced its roadworthiness.

All of these elements came along to the production Dyna line in 2007, but the bigger news that year was the Twin Cam engine. With the 96-inch engine becoming standard for all of the production touring models in 2007, of course the CVO motorcycle team had to step up the game for their limited-production Screamin' Eagle bikes. By tweaking the motor with 4-inch bore and new forged pistons, displacement climbed to 110 cubic inches, making it H-D's largest displacement production engine ever; just the ticket for the 2007 Screamin' Eagle factory customs. Think about that: a 110 motor delivering 105 foot-pounds of torque in a Dyna motorcycle? That's right. And weighing in at almost 200 pounds *less* than its big brother, the CVO Ultra Classic motorcycle, the Dyna motorcycle took command of the road with no fear and maximum moxie.

Harley-Davidson offered the 2007 CVO Screamin' Eagle Dyna Low Rider motorcycle in Inferno Red and Desert Black (top), Silver Rush and Midnight Black (bottom), and Twilight Blue and Ice Blue Pearl (opposite page).

According to a review in *Motorcyclist,*

> Since most of those pounds are situated close to the pavement, steering effort is refreshingly light despite chopperesque steering geometry. As opposed to the fashionably phat rubber on other upscale factory customs, a sane, 170mm-wide rear tire helps handling everywhere. The 43mm inverted fork does a worthy job of keeping that skinny front tire accurately aimed.

Did he say "inverted" fork? Yes, indeed. The factory custom design team set out to give the Screamin' Eagle Dyna motorcycle a super-low and stretched pro-street look by fitting up inverted forks and forged aluminum triple clamps, among other things. The chrome upside-down forks were available in the P&A catalog from which the CVO motorcycle team often drew components to show owners how to enhance their own bikes. In this instance, the inverted fork fit the aggressive, street-going style of the Screamin' Eagle Dyna motorcycle.

All Harley-Davidson motorcycles had electronic fuel injection (EFI) by 2007, a change that had been accommodated in Dyna motorcycles back in 2004 when a longer fuel tank came on board to allow what was then an option. CVO motorcycle paint designers took full advantage of the larger palette, too, making the most of the sheet metal with three dynamic color combinations that suited the Dyna motorcycle's personality: Silver Rush and Midnight Black; Inferno Red and Desert Black; and Twilight Blue with Ice Blue Pearl and Granite.

With its yellow frame, the 2008 CVO Fat Bob motorcycle was arguably the most eye-catching CVO model to date.

The FXDSE model shows off that handsome front rolling stock.

As always, nothing is left to chance when a Screamin' Eagle model greets the world: cohesive design integration is paramount. The Screamin' Eagle Dyna motorcycle strutted a color-matched frame, chin spoiler, battery box, electrical panel cover, coil cover, and swingarm. Gleaming chrome covers major components front to back, featuring that robust front end, new straight cut mufflers with full-length chrome covers, struts, and chrome-covered shocks complete with hand-adjustable preload. The list of shiny stuff continues with plenty of parts from P&A's Knurled Accessory Collection, including footpegs, shift peg, brake pedal pad, grips, axle nut covers, and more. And let's not overlook the Chrome Road Winder Forged Aluminum custom wheels with matching rotors and chrome sprocket—as if one could.

Other trick parts that join in to make a bike even more special are the spun-aluminum, metal-faced speedometer and mini tachometer, along with a chromed fuel cap with hidden LEDs that light up to show levels when the bike is turned on.

For Harley-Davidson's 105th Anniversary year in 2008, the FXDSE2 model returned as a custom factory machine, along with the other three models repeating from 2007. All of them benefitted from distinctive, serialized Anniversary paint and accessory

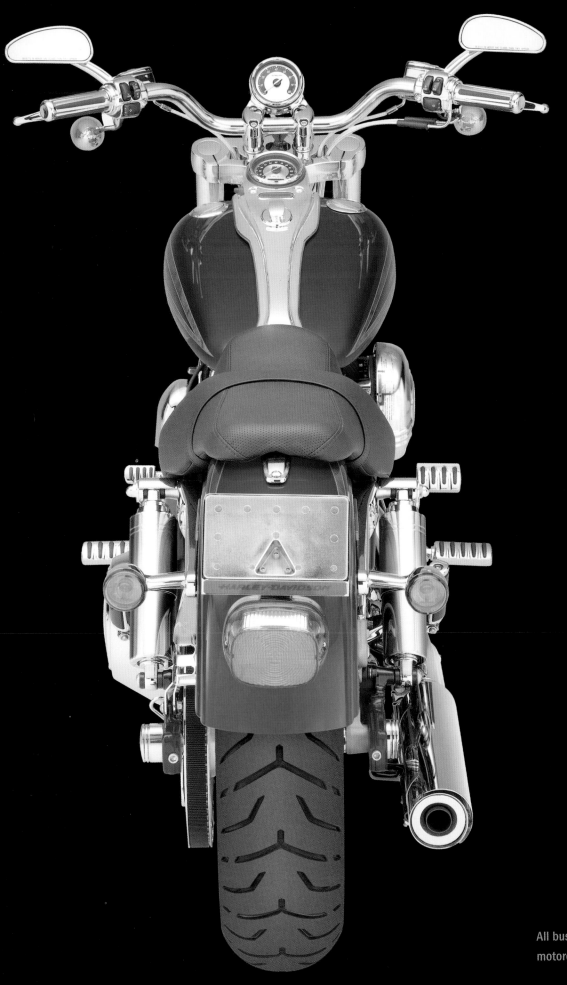

All business in the rider's seat of the FXDSE
motorcycle.

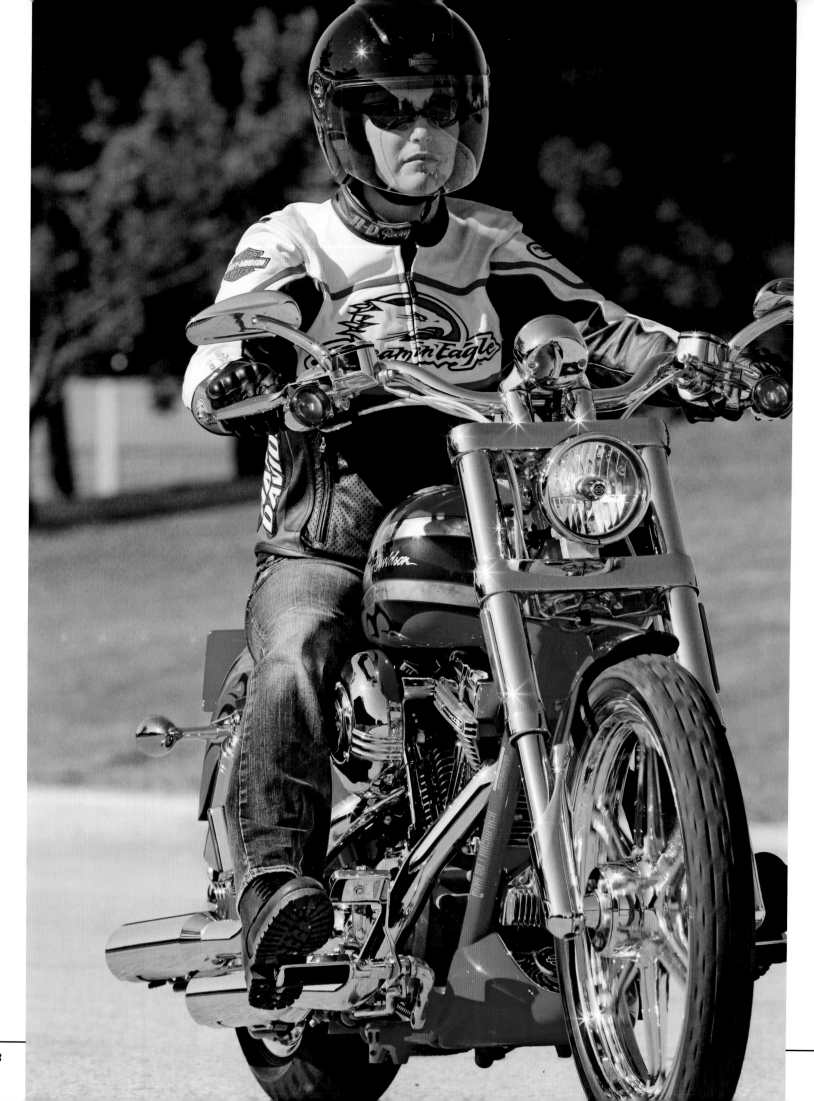

packages that included Crystal Copper and Black Onyx paint trimmed in gold leaf and a cloisonné medallion. But don't be fooled into thinking there were few differences for this model year. As Terry Roorda of *Thunder Press* stated of the 2008 CVO models that they "are returnees in name only. Cosmetically and functionally, all four models received extensive revisions, some of them quite dramatic."

Those changes manifested in the Dyna motorcycle mainly in terms of handling characteristics. The aggressive pro-street attitude offered by the inverted fork in the previous year went in for alterations in steering geometry and rider position. The rake was tucked in to 29 degrees and an inch was taken off the front suspension height. A redesigned, perforated leather seat and a repositioning of the 1.25-inch handlebars placed the rider in a closer, more upright location. These changes hit the mark, offering vastly improved comfort and control and making the motorcycle a more potent canyon carver than before, especially with the 110 engine in charge.

The engine stayed essentially the same on the inside but keeping with the concept of anniversary decorations it was treated to special finishing on the outside. Granite powder-coating on the cases, incorporating flecks of stainless steel, added texture and subtle sheen to the powerplant while emphasizing its inherent capabilities. It breathes through a low-restriction air cleaner and strums out a throaty exhaust tone, compliments of the staggered shorty dual exhaust and straight-cut mufflers with full-length chrome covers. It's just stunning.

OPPOSITE:
The custom details on CVO motorcycles turn heads on any road.

BELOW:
Anniversary years made for some of the most exclusive CVO machines to date.

Simple, robust, and loaded with class.

P&A's Stealth collection was sourced for the footpegs, shift peg, brake pedal pads, and hand controls. A slick and shiny new tank console allowed the relocation of gauges and functional components, holding the ignition switch and a larger 4-inch speedometer, moved here from the handlebars. Replacing the speedometer on the bars is a 4-inch, spun aluminum tachometer. The bars, by the way, are now adjustable and internally wired for sanitary good looks and rider comfort.

Gleaming prettily in their own right are mirror chrome Slotted 6-Spoke wheels, P&A mainstays that have occasionally turned up on special models due to their elegant essence. Here, they've been hand-polished to amp up the dazzle. The 21-inch front sports a slim, trim fender that's held in place by those inverted forks. The 17-inch rear is shod with a capable 170mm tire.

The paint pattern carries through from the sheet metal to the battery box, coil cover, and electrical panel, further enhanced by the color-matched chin spoiler, frame, swing arm, and air-cleaner insert. In addition to the 105th Anniversary color scheme of Crystal Copper and Black Onyx, other options include Candy Cobalt with Midnight Blue; and Scarlet Red Pearl with Dark Crimson.

Oddly, while the design team saw the inverted fork as a leading attribute of the 2007 and 2008 Screamin' Eagle Dyna motorcycles, it was among the least noticed, overshadowed perhaps by the 110 engine. Apparently Screamin' Eagle Dyna motorcycle riders were gone from the curb far too quickly to talk about styling innovations. That said, it's this sort of unsung virtue, unheralded in its time, that bodes well for later recognition. Owners of Screamin' Eagle Dyna motorcycles from these years had best hold on to their motorcycles. For more reasons than one, they have "future classic" stamped into their DNA.

FXDFSE CVO DYNA FAT BOB MODEL

In 2009, the tenth year of Harley-Davidson's limited production, factory custom program, model names were finally adapted to include "CVO" in their titles. H-D had used the designation to describe the program itself for several years by then, but model names had retained the Screamin' Eagle nomenclature in recognition of the engine performance upgrades these motorcycles touted.

As it happened, 2009 was the Fat Bob motorcycle's first CVO model makeover opportunity, having just joined the Dyna production lineup the year before. And what a makeover it was! In fact, the CVO Fat Bob motorcycle is probably the most daring metamorphosis ever accomplished by CVO motorcycle designers and engineers. Why? Because the year of the Fat Bob motorcycle's OE release was also the year of H-D's introduction of the Dark Custom lineup. The Fat Bob motorcycle was one of this series of blacked-out, retro-vibed Sportster, Dyna, and Softail models envisioned to appeal to a younger demographic while simultaneously harkening back to styling cues from

The FX chassis is the traditional mount for back roads, and attention from the CVO motorcycle team only makes it better.

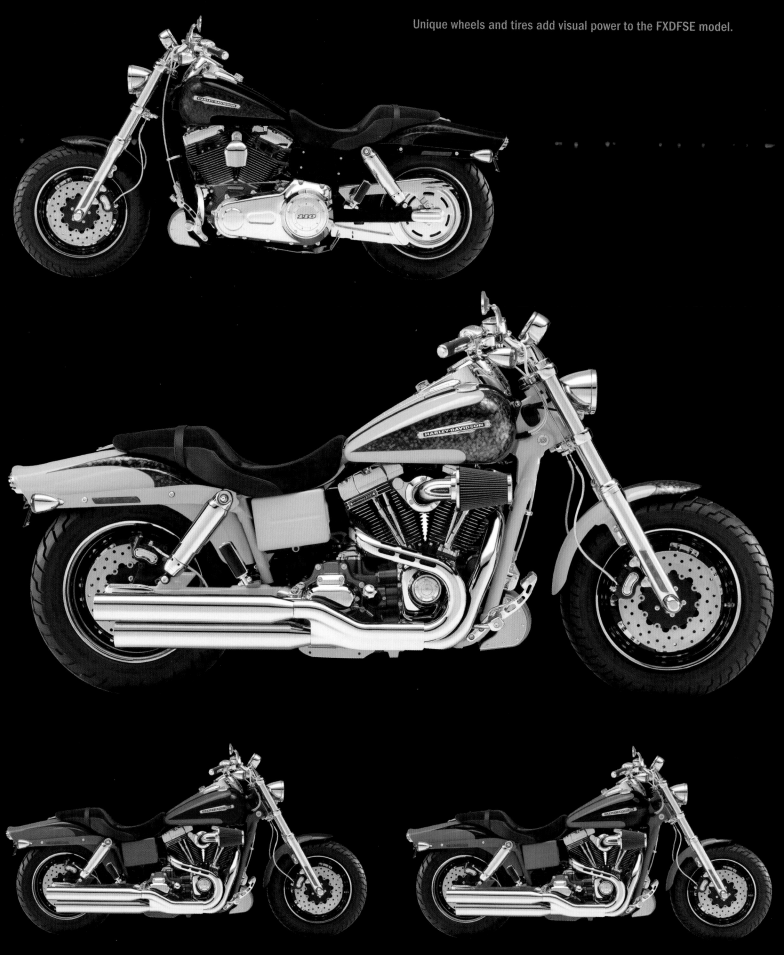

Unique wheels and tires add visual power to the FXDFSE model.

CVO motorcycles get bold, contrasting paintwork other motorcycles can only dream of.

Every flavor of orange looks good on a Harley-Davidson CVO motorcycle.

Harley's earlier times. The Fat Bob motorcycle was configured as a stripped-down street fighter with an aggressive stance and chubby countenance. Reminiscent of traditional post-war bobbers and the seven Dark Custom bikes, the Fat Bob motorcycle distinguished itself as the only model that springboarded to the CVO roster. It did so the very next year and, in the process, was transformed from grim gothic skulker to bling-bedazzled showstopper.

Not all of the OE Fat Bob motorcycles were dressed as Dark Custom models, but most of the offered paint options featured matte "denim" paint or solid, subdued colors. And if you know anything about the CVO motorcycle program, you know that "paint" and "subdued" never appear in the same sentence when describing these bikes. So when the CVO motorcycle team took on the job of tarting up the Fat Bob motorcycle, they were challenged to blend the best of both worlds. One result was the first-ever combination of matte and gloss paint finishes on a CVO model: Denim Granite with Electric Blue Fade. Other choices were: Black Diamond and Fire Quartz; Sunrise Yellow Pearl and Platinum Quartz; and Electric Orange and Slate Black. Mission accomplished: the 2009 CVO Fat Bob model emerged consistent with the model's overall demeanor, yet became another strong motorcycle in the CVO lineup.

But don't think paint treatments tell the whole story of the Fat Bob motorcycle makeover. That's because the CVO motorcycle formula always includes more in the engine compartment and more in the parts department, too; this just as true for this fattened up Dyna motorcycle as for any model in the program.

The Fat Bob motorcycle was a distinctive bike from its 2008 OE release featuring signature twin headlights on a hefty 49mm front end, chrome-covered shocks, and bobbed rear fender. The hefty 5.1-gallon fuel tank, Cruise Drive six-speed transmission, and two-into-one exhaust with staggered dual mufflers contributed function and range.

Fat Bob motorcycles don't need flashy paint to exude presence, but it doesn't hurt.

ABOVE:
A custom intake and detailed flame graphics lend a hot rod flair.

Bill Davidson shares the stage with the commanding CVO Fat Bob motorcycle in 2009.

The CVO Fat Bob motorcycle is kicked up with brand-new 16-inch Fang wheels, front and back, that with black powder-coated, slotted centers and chrome inserts around the rim. The wheels are appropriately covered with meaty-treaded tires: a 180 on the rear and *a 130 on the front*—the largest ever on a Dyna motorcycle.

Dyna motorcycles already had a reputation for agile handling and exhilarating performance, and the Fat Bob motorcycle scores high in that regard. A slightly shorter wheelbase and reasonable 28-degree fork angle combine with lowered and retuned suspension front and rear for spirited riding.

Of course much of the rider's experience is due to the response and power of the fuel-injected Screamin' Eagle Twin Cam 110 engine, tweaked with the popular Heavy Breather air cleaner and freer-flowing mufflers. Said Billy Bartels in a review on *MotorcycleCruiser.com*, "The 110-inch Twin Cam motor is perfectly matched to this 725 lb. bike to make it a real hoot to ride."

The engine looks as beautiful as it runs, finished in granite powder-coat and dressed up in chrome covers. Other concessions to appearance include braided steel lines, chromed fork sliders, smoked LED rear light assembly, and the first-ever use of

For people looking for a more subdued color scheme, Harley-Davidson offered the 2009 CVO Fat Bob motorcycle in this Black Diamond and Fire Quartz livery.

Alcantara synthetic suede on a Harley-Davidson seat. Fatter flat track-style handle-bars with internal wiring clean up the front. The intuitive color matching procedure on frame, swingarm, and battery box are also incorporated in the custom dash this time.

When the Fat Bob motorcycle returned for its encore in the 2010 CVO lineup, it continued to live large, outfitted with new paint schemes, the 110 Twin Cam engine, and tons of chrome: in short, everything riders loved about the 2009 iteration and then some.

One subtle addition is the Midnight Pearl plating placed here and there, including the dual-headlight nacelles, taillight cover, fender struts, and various smaller covers. It's the kind of thing that's rarely pointed out, but it discreetly and elegantly contributes to the overall package.

This stealthy pearl-finish plating works in concert with accessories from P&A's Diamond Black Collection, a line of satin-black components that feature contrast sections of raw aluminum—the perfect choice for the CVO Fat Bob motorcycle. Among the components from the collection that quietly blend in are footpegs, shifter peg, grips, and brake pedal pad. The speedometer and tachometer are embellished with Diamond Black faces.

A more design element is the new two-piece, distressed-leather seat that gets high marks not only for its proper good looks but for comfort, too.

These design cues—the pearl plating, the Diamond Black accessories, and the brown leather seat—are perfect foils for the 2010 Fat Bob motorcycle's paint and graphics, especially the Satin Pewter with Sandstorm Grind, which features the return of metal grind accents as found on several Softail CVO models as early as 2005. Two other color choices: Cryptic Black with Hellfire Flames, and Opal Blue with Hellfire Flames are abundant in sophisticated detail as well.

No doubt about it, the CVO motorcycle team pulled out the stops transforming a ready-to-rumble bobber into a proper profiler with the CVO Fat Bob motorcycle, a machine that not only has the looks to pull it off but the chops to sustain the performance. The cool thing about the Fat Bob motorcycle is the way its styling stays true to the spirit established by H-D's early factory customs. Keeping pace with technology may be necessary, but keeping in touch with tradition feeds the soul.

In 2010, Harley-Davidson highlighted the Cryptic Black paint of the CVO Dyna Fat Bob motorcycle with Hellfire flames.

ABOVE:
A muscular profile lends visual power to the CVO Fat Bob motorcycle.

LEFT:
Luscious brown leather saddles are just another standout feature on the CVO Fat Bob motorcycle.

CHAPTER 4

The Deuce was always a desirable motorcycle; a CVO model only made it more so.

SOFTAIL MOTORCYCLES: RETRO CVO MODELS

FXSTDSE SCREAMIN' EAGLE SOFTAIL DEUCE & FXSTDSE 2 SCREAMIN' EAGLE SOFTAIL DEUCE MODELS

Ah, the Deuce motorcyle . . . it's impossible not to wax poetic about this motorcycle, even in stock trim. But talk about the Screamin' Eagle factory custom version of the Deuce motorcycle, in *100th Anniversary* trim, no less, and even the most seasoned, stony, stalwart rider swoons!

LEFT:
From the front, the rakish presence of the Screamin' Eagle Softail Deuce model is unmistakable.

According to Jim Hofman, who was managing the factory custom program at the time of its development, "That was and still is, in my opinion, one of the most beautiful and comprehensive bikes Harley-Davidson has ever developed. If you look at that bike and you go through the details, it's just amazing. From the gold leaf paint to every little tiny thing."

From the first production model released in 1999, the Deuce motorcycle was a standout, dubbed by Kevin Wing of *motorcyclecruiser.com* "the best-looking full production motorcycle gracing any showroom." In fact, some described the Softail Deuce motorcycle as a radical bike; assembly-line motorcycles didn't *look* like this at the turn of the millennium. By the time the anniversary year rolled around, there was a consensus at the Motor Company: it was time to turn the factory custom limelight on the Softail Deuce motorcycle. And there would be nothing mild about the approach.

With the rousing success of the Screamin' Eagle Road Glide, Road King, and Dyna Wide Glide motorcycles in the first several years of the limited production factory custom program, Harley motorcycle riders made it apparent that there was room in the market and room in their hearts for these special edition models. And though the program's designers and engineers had yet to put a motorcycle from the Softail platform under the knife, it was Harley-Davidson's 100th Anniversary year. What better time for the Deuce motorcycle, a confirmed jewel in the crown, to sparkle with intent?

It's been said that the Deuce motorcycle was also a jewel in the mind of Willie G., and that's a brilliant affirmation worth noting. Because when it came time to bring the Deuce motorcycle into the fold as a factory custom, it was Willie G., the head of H-D Styling, who was deeply involved in guiding the CVO motorcycle team. And it shows.

The Motor Company had a big year in 2003, and the Screamin' Eagle Softail Deuce model marked the occasion perfectly.

The Screamin' Eagle Softail Deuce model was twice as nice as the already excellent Softail Deuce model.

Pull up on a Deuce motorcycle and the first thing you'll hear is, "Man, that's a beautiful motorcycle." Get used to it, too, because that's a comment Screamin' Eagle Softail Deuce motorcycle owners hear over and over again. You might even begin to wonder if the word "beautiful" was coined specifically to describe this bike, they're so often linked in the same sentence. The only thing wrong with this characterization is the way it sidesteps the power and performance of this beauty; the bike does indeed exhibit *both* of those traits, in spades.

Yes, the 2003 Screamin' Eagle Deuce motorcycle was the first Softail model to be selected for factory custom treatment. Further, the FXSTDSE model was also the first Softail model ever to be blessed with a 95 cubic inch Twin Cam engine, quite a sizeable powerplant. Before 2003, this 1550cc motor had been reserved only for rubber-mounted touring models, the likes of the Road King and the Road Glide motorcycles. Until the Screamin' Eagle Deuce motorcycle, that is. When the 2003 FXSTDSE model hit the road with that big motor and its trimmed-down livery, compared to the touring bikes, it quite literally took off. Weighing in at 712 pounds wet (677 dry), the Screamin' Eagle Deuce motorcycle touted a power-to-weight ratio that left others in the dust.

Let's get down to brass tacks: the 1550cc Twin Cam big-bore engine features top-of-the-line Electronic Sequential Port Fuel Injection, a 9.4:1 compression ratio, and 91 foot pounds of torque. This bests the 8.8:1 compression and 85 foot pounds of torque in the Twin Cam 88B engine. And this balanced engine isn't just powerful, it's pretty as well, finished off in silver and chrome. The five-speed constant mesh transmission features double-row chain and Poly chain belt for solid reliable shifts.

Of course, part of any Softail motorcycle's appeal is the way it hides the rear shock to masquerade as a hardtail, giving the look of old-school cred. Further accentuating this model's low, sleek lines is low profile front and rear suspension, yielding a seat

height that's an inch lower. Speaking of seats, that's another notable attribute of the Screamin' Eagle Deuce motorcycle: those chrome trim strips built into the low-profile seat and pillion. Word is this was a challenge for the supplier tasked to figure it out, but they did it.

The 2003 FXSTDSE model steps out in only one-color combination, and it's a stunner: Centennial Gold and Vivid Black with Gold Leaf Graphics. Many parts are color-matched to the Centennial Gold frame—it *is* the Anniversary Edition, after all. These include the swingarm, timer, derby cover, fuel tank console inserts, modified teardrop style air cleaner trim, and front spoiler. The distinctive air cleaner, we should mention, was developed specifically for this motorcycle and it sold in the tens of thousands when it hit the P&A catalog. And that neat, sleek, tucked-in chin spoiler, by the way, was one of several items that Harley's Styling Department (read: Willie G.) insisted on for this motorcycle. One glance confirms that it was the right touch in the totally right place.

No detail was forgotten. Case in point: both front and rear wheel bearing spacers are unique to this motorcycle. They were machined to include the proper radius, then chrome plated just for the Deuce motorcycle. Chrome Slotted Six Spoke wheels, 21-inch front and 17-inch rear, roll along with matching chrome Slotted Six Spoke rear sprocket and floating brake rotors. Reeling in this beefy beauty with appropriate style are dual front disc brakes, as opposed to the production model's single, with splendid silver brake calipers bearing billet-style chrome inserts.

A smaller item, such as the rear brake lever, might be overlooked or considered insignificant on another motorcycle; not on the Screamin' Eagle Softail Deuce motorcycle. To be just right, the lever needed to have a radius embedded in the middle of it, which required a unique forging; that is precisely what it got.

The details on a Harley-Davidson are clean, but CVO models take refinement to another level.

And notice the chrome piece that bridges the usual gap between the risers. The chrome tachometer cup nests nicely there. Also adding to the clean lines up front is a fat 1 ¼-inch diameter handlebar with internal wiring. The bars are elegantly dressed up with chrome Bullet mirrors, Aileron custom grips, Buckshot chrome brake and clutch hand controls, and brake master cylinder, clutch lever, and switch housings—all in chrome, naturally.

Custom cues include clear-coated, braided stainless control cables and brake lines. And we haven't even talked about all the attention given to the foot controls! The list goes on, but if you're the kind of rider who notices and appreciates deftly applied detail, you don't mind at all, right?

"It was an incredible effort," added Hofman. "Everything Styling wanted on this motorcycle was delivered, at much expense and effort." And don't forget, with striking results, too.

The 100th Anniversary Badges on the fuel tank console and crankcase of the 2003 Screamin' Eagle Deuce motorcycle are dead giveaways that it's the celebration-year Screamin' Eagle version of the model. For 2004, the Screamin' Eagle Softail Deuce motorcycle remained in the factory custom program lineup as the FXSTDSE 2 model. Retaining the singular detailing of its predecessor, the 2004 version sported new pin-striped, graphic-embellished color choices and a slew of additional custom details.

The lowered look persists, with dropped suspension front and rear and the low-slung, chrome-accented leather seat and pillion. Over/under shotgun dual exhaust system returns compete with chrome heat shields, as do dual front disc brakes with silver brake calipers and billet-style chrome inserts. Sparkling rolling stock includes chrome Detonator three-spoke custom wheels, 21-inch front and 17-inch rear, with matching Detonator three-spoke floating brake rotors and rear sprocket. The180mm rear tire gives the term "chubby" a positive connotation.

In the beauty department, components color-matched to the frame include not only the swingarm, struts, and oil tank, but also that very distinctive chin spoiler, fuel tank console, and frame inserts. Painting the lower frame rails has a subtle but impactful result, outlining the silver-and-chrome 1550cc fuel-injected Twin Cam 95B engine in color, making the motorcycle feel more compact, more complete. This design approach isn't particular to the Screamin' Eagle Deuce motorcycle, it just works so very well on this motorcycle.

For this year, the model was dressed in two different but equally evocative outfits, Yellow Pearl and Platinum Mist; and Candy Cobalt and Starlight Black. In both cases, the sassy stylized teardrop air cleaner features spun-aluminum inserts. Continuing the theme are the machine-turned silver metallic speedometer face and matching riser-mounted mini-tachometer with its tapered cover.

Like the 2003 Screamin' Eagle Deuce motorcycle, this model has chrome forward control mounting brackets, polished Bullet stainless shift linkage, chrome Bullet shift and rear brake levers, and Aileron chrome and rubber footpegs, brake pedal pad, and shifter peg. But here's one important change for the 2004 model year: EFI became standard on the Deuce motorcycle in 2003, but in 2004, other Softail models received the upgrade as well. A happy addition to this and every bike in the 2004 model year: a two-year factory warranty.

Some riders think of the Deuce model as the motorcyclists' motorcycle, one to be appreciated only by the most discerning among us. Like many artists, the Screamin' Eagle Softail Deuce motorcycle was perhaps misunderstood in its own time, judging from several unenlightened reviews. But it's that very sensibility that is sure to guarantee the model's destiny as a bona fide classic, especially since only about 3,000 were built. And though the word "Deuce" implies more than one—*two* to be precise—take it from those who own and ride this motorcycle: there's only *one* Deuce motorcycle, and it's a custom cruiser with no peer.

FLSTFSE SCREAMIN' EAGLE FAT BOY MOTORCYCLE

When the Fat Boy motorcycle appeared on showroom floors in 1990, it was an unqualified success, and not just in Harley-Davidson circles. It obliterated expectations in the worldwide cruiser bike scene, as well.

Why? Well, first of all, Willie G. designed it, ensuring incomparable cachet. Second, it was built on the Softail platform, meaning hidden shocks provided a hardcore, hardtail appearance mated to the comfort of modern suspension. But what really set the Fat Boy motorcycle apart was the way it *looked*. The most identifiable features are those solid aluminum wheels front and rear. Then there's the wide fuel tank and beefy front end; next, add the substantial tires, with their even more substantial fenders. Yes, this Boy gave "fat" new connotations. Remember, this was 1990: no other Harley motorcycle, no other cruising motorcycle on the market *anywhere*, looked like this!

Because it only came in gray when first released as a production bike, the Fat Boy motorcycle was nicknamed "The Grey Ghost." But it didn't take long for the Ghost to step out of the shadows; the Fat Boy motorcycle soon garnered notice from mainstream pop culture and turned up everywhere. Once actor Arnold Schwarzenegger saddled up on a Fat Boy in the 1991 movie *Terminator 2: Judgment Day*, the model's icon status was assured.

In 2005 Harley-Davidson offered the Screamin' Eagle Fat Boy model in Platinum Mist and Slate (top), Electric Cherry and Vivid Black (bottom), and Candy Cobalt and Starlight Black (opposite page).

So if the production Fat Boy motorcycle was a super star in motorcycling's firmament, then certainly the Screamin' Eagle version would not disappoint. And it didn't. But considering its initial groundbreaking status, you might wonder why Harley-Davidson waited until 2005, the model's fifteenth-anniversary year, to give the Fat Boy motorcycle factory custom attention. When it bowed to the press, its reception was so effusive and the demand so great that the models' wheels barely touched showroom floors before rolling home with happy owners.

Delighted, one reviewer at *powersportsnetwork.com* wrote: "The Harley-Davidson Custom Vehicle Operations (CVO) crew has infused the new 2005 limited-edition FLSTFSE Screamin' Eagle Fat Boy with rowdy performance and a lean, urban custom profile."

Cycle World labeled the 2005 CVO Fat Boy motorcycle the best cruiser motorcycle of the year, writing, "Simply put, this limited-edition factory custom is as close to cruiser perfection as anything we've ridden."

That's high praise indeed. More compelling, the CVO motorcycle release event in 2005 that included the Fat Boy motorcycle—along with the year's two other CVO models, the Screamin' Eagle Electra Glide, and Screamin' Eagle V-Rod models—invited moto-journalists to tear down the eighth-mile at Irwindale Dragstrip near Los Angeles on the bikes. The event resulted in such gushing compliments and exuberant reviews that the moto-press corps still talk about it to this day. When you get such superlatives from some of the most demanding riders on earth—testing a street model on a dragstrip no less—you're doing something right.

Like the original factory Fat Boy motorcycle, the 2005 CVO Fat Boy motorcycle does a *ton* of things right. Starting with the seat of power, the 2005 CVO Fat Boy motorcycle features a 1690cc balanced Twin Cam 103B engine. Topping out at 17 percent greater displacement than the production model, it's the largest engine offered to date in a production Harley-Davidson motorcycle. According to *Cycle World*, the engine offers "an impressive boost in power and torque over the standard 88-incher."

The extra oomph inherent in the Fat Boy motorcycle's hand-built engine comes compliments of Stroker flywheels, 3.875-inch diameter pistons, and big-bore cylinders, all sourced from the Screamin' Eagle line of performance parts. Screamin' Eagle heads are beautifully finished in silver powder-coat and topped with chrome covers. Not surprisingly, turning over a stroker engine takes extra kick, so a heavy-duty 1.4 kilowatt starter is on board. To help the beast breathe, there's a Stage 1 Screamin' Eagle air cleaner with new teardrop-style cover and slash-down exhaust with chrome heat shields. Sequential Port Fuel-Injection, with its clean, precise throttle response, is retained from the production bike, but a heavy-duty hydraulic clutch is added. The engine is tuned to crank out more than 100 foot pounds of torque—quite impressive for a 50-state-compliant motorcycle.

Rolling stock and binders are a large part of the bike's visual and functional appeal. Who doesn't remark on those the striking polished aluminum disc wheels? Sanitary looks are aided by internally wired, 1 ¼-inch-wide handlebars atop the raked-out neck and chromed front end. Single floating rotors ride both front and rear, and standard four-piston calipers sparkle with tasteful silver finish and chrome inserts. The matching disc wheel out back is fit with the proper pulley setup, of course, and the curve hugging is aided by lowered rear suspension.

The Fat Boy motorcycle's metal-edged seat also draws constant comments. In terms of design flow, it's the perfect complement to the 2005 Fat Boy motorcycle's paint and graphics treatment because this is the first CVO model to use sheet metal

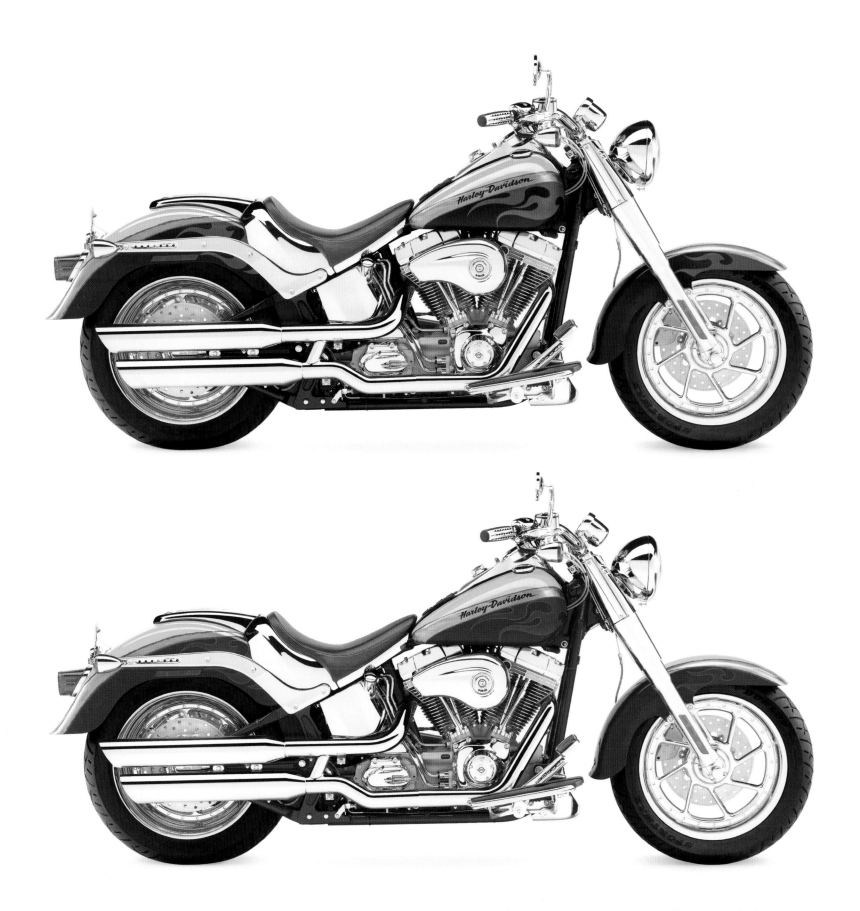

accented with the metal grind process. When the team was dredging up ideas for the CVO Fat Boy motorcycle, something ingenious and outstanding was in order because, as everyone knows, paint is such a statement. Jim Hofman even had metal grind flames on his personal bike, a 2001 Fat Boy motorcycle that had been customized at a local Milwaukee shop. Was that an option?

Harley-Davidson offered the 2006 Screamin' Eagle Fat Boy motorcycle in Canyon Copper and Concord Purple (opposite), Autumn Haze and Abyss Blue (top), and Nebula Yellow and Cobalt Blue (bottom).

Metal grind is a process in which patterns are etched or ground into the raw steel, then left visible, sealed, and clear-coated to protect and preserve them. That description makes the process sound easy, but it's nothing of the kind. When raw metal is machine-etched, it wants to rust almost immediately, at the touch of a finger. In a one-off situation this can be handled, but remember: as "custom" as the CVO line is, it's also "custom production," meaning that several thousand motorcycles are being built simultaneously. According to Hofman, "It was very challenging to paint that grind in a production environment. When you're doing a couple thousand for Harley-Davidson customers there's a high expectation of long term durability, as there should be."

A solution was found while working with Calibre, Inc., a Grafton, Wisconsin, paint supplier to Harley-Davidson. The panels were ground, immediately clear-coated, then moved on to color-coat applications, and the panels were again clear-coated. The results are nothing short of stunning, evidenced by the repeated use of the process on other CVO models after this, not to mention lavish customer praise. The 2005 Screamin' Eagle Fat Boy motorcycle makes sparks fly in more ways than one.

Three different color combinations took the stage that year: Two-Tone Electric Cherry and Vivid Black, Two-Tone Candy Cobalt and Starlight Black, and Two-Tone Platinum Mist and Slate. No matter which one you prefer, the look is undeniably industrial while dead-on elegant at the same time. It carries through from front to rear fender, thanks to additional steely touchstones that include braided stainless cables, spun-aluminum metal-faced gauges, and, of course, the distinctive, decorative chrome pillion that draws your eye along the bike's lines.

Finally, factor in more than 50 chromed, polished, drilled, braided, or etched components—along with Harley-Davidson's on-board security system and a special CVO motorcycle key and storage cover—and you reach that pinnacle of quality and expectation that marks these motorcycles as undeniably premium.

The 2006 FLSTFSE 2 Screamin' Eagle Fat Boy motorcycle strutted into showrooms with many of the same touches, but on new rolling stock in the form of Dunlop 140mm front and 200mm rear tires. The beefier rubber is right at home on bigger 17-inch forged aluminum Road Winder wheels, kicked up from the 2005 model's 16-inch ones and still as distinctive as ever. This change necessitated widening of the frame, fenders, and strut covers, adding even further to the fat-is-beautiful look, which was further emphasized by the Fat Boy model's lowered rear suspension.

The design team didn't waste a millimeter of those wide fenders, either, using the additional real estate to get creative, as you'd expect. Ghost flames were added to metal grind accents that are candy-color-coated this time for a looking-glass glimpse of over-the-top custom cool.

Back was the Screamin' Eagle 103 Stroker Twin Cam engine with EFI, hydraulic clutch, and Stage 1 teardrop-style air cleaner for an encore performance—and why not? As the largest displacement motor in a production bike, this stroked monster has proven itself with more than 96 foot pounds of torque at 4,000 RPM and smooth street performance featuring unhinged power on tap at the twist of the throttle. It's as striking as ever, powder-coated in silver and dressed up in chrome covers.

The color choices for 2006 were Autumn Haze and Abyss Blue, Nebula Yellow and Cobalt Blue, and Concord Purple and Canyon Copper. Would-be owners were encouraged to indulge the fantasy and pick a favorite, but warned not to dally. The FLSTFSE Screamin' Eagle Fat Boy motorcycle, a favorite among favorites, would not be denied its due.

FXSTSSE SCREAMIN' EAGLE/CVO SOFTAIL SPRINGER MODEL

Harley-Davidson offered the Screamin' Eagle Softail Springer motorcycle in Canyon Copper and Candy Red for the 2007 model year.

More than any other motorcycle component you could name, a Springer motorcycle front end, with its head-turning, nostalgia-inducing, commanding presence simply screams "retro." And even though springers first appeared on Harley-Davidson motorcycles as early as 1930, when most riders today think of Springer motorcycles, they think of bikes built decades *after* that time: the choppers of the 1960s and 1970s. This phenomenon is even more curious considering the Motor Company didn't build a single model with a Springer motorcycle front end between the years of 1949 and 1987, bringing it back only sporadically through the years.

Yet there's no denying the appeal of motorcycles with Springer motorcycles, and you'll find their allure especially powerful among traditional grassroots riders. Diehards might tell you that a Springer motorcycle front end on a Softail motorcycle is a mixed metaphor, but the practical among us would say there's no better model than a Softail—with its hidden suspension out back—to sport a Springer motorcycle front end. The Softail motorcycle and the Springer motorcycle front end just might be the optimal combination for a spirited ride back to the heady days of old-school American motorcycling.

For 2008 Harley-Davidson added Black Diamond with Smoked Candy flames to the color palate for the CVO Softail Springer motorcycle.

CVO models have always been blessed with eye-grabbing custom wheels in striking sizes.

Springer motorcycles appeared three times in succession over the span of Harley-Davidson's custom vehicle program, moving there from the OE line-up. The first year was the 2007 Screamin' Eagle Softail Springer motorcycle, before the CVO designation was coined to name these limited production bikes. The second time the Softail Springer motorcycle received custom factory treatment was in 2008, Harley-Davidson's 105th Anniversary model year. That time, the Softail Springer motorcycle gave a whole new definition to "bedecked and bedazzled." The Springer motorcycle's hat trick was the 2009 CVO Softail Springer motorcycle, after CVO motorcycle terminology has entered the H-D lexicon. In every iteration, the FXSTSSE Softail Springer is a motorcycle standout.

Mentioning the FXSTSSE model revealed a soft spot with Jim Hofman: "Ah, these were beautiful bikes," he said. "Beautiful wheels and a gorgeous cast aluminum oil tank with fins that were chrome plated. And the Heavy Breather air cleaner is still big today. We plucked it from P&A and it added a very unique look to this bike."

As visually stunning as these three models are, owners will tell you they're not for everyone. Then again, consistent with the mandate to provide premium custom motorcycles in exclusive editions for the most enlightened riders, no CVO model is made for the mainstream. But Springer motorcycles especially require more of a rider: more alertness, more body English, and more engagement. Framed in these terms, the Springer Softail motorcycle is the ideal platform choice for the CVO motorcycle program. CVO motorcycles, after all, always have more of everything.

The year 2009 was the last year for the CVO Springer Softail motorcycle.

The 2007 CVO Springer Softail motorcycle was as close as a rider could get to a bespoke custom and still have a factory warranty.

Besides Canyon Copper and Candy Red,
Harley-Davidson offered the 2007 Screamin'
Eagle Softail Springer motorcycle in Abyss
Blue and Blue Pearl (top) and Amarillo Gold
and Candy Tangerine (bottom).

For their first stab at souping up a Springer motorcycle, the H-D CVO motorcycle team knew they'd have to balance both the visual and actual weight of the leading link Springer fork. There was a 21-inch Revolver 10-spoke forged aluminum front wheel to consider, too. Harmony was accomplished with a wide 200mm rear tire on a flashy 17-inch matching Revolver rear wheel—chromed like the front one, of course. Lowered rear suspension and dropped seat height add to its curb-hugging stance.

Conscientiously chosen, color-matched parts contribute to a cohesive package that riffs off the powder-coated frame. These include the Springer motorcycle's rigid forks and upper triple clamp, the oil tank, seat post, muffler support bracket, and swingarm.

Sure all this bling is distracting, but the FXSTSSE model, like all of the Screamin' Eagle limited editions this year, got major attention in the power department as well. The cases of H-D's stellar 95 cubic inch Twin Cam engine were bored out to 110 and topped with high-compression heads that sport larger intake valves. Yes, low-RPM torque got a healthy performance bump. The Softail model's counterbalanced 110B engine was further tweaked with Screamin' Eagle tuning parts, such as chrome shotgun slash down mufflers. A classy, round air cleaner sits front and center.

Wait, though: there's more shiny stuff, such as a plethora of parts from H-D P&A's new Centerline Collection. Rider and passenger foot pegs, grips, brake and shift levers, shift linkage, shifter peg, and more feature-thick stripes of chrome contrasted with black. The chrome mini-tachometer and mount fit nicely behind a chrome headlight nacelle. One of the coolest bits is the plain-looking fuel tank cap; not till you start up the bike do you see the row of LEDs that display the fuel level in the cap.

Gilding the lily further are three rarified paint schemes: Amarillo Gold and Candy Tangerine with hand-painted Tribal Flame graphics; Abyss Blue and Blue Pearl with hand-painted Tribal Flame graphics; and Canyon Copper and Candy Red with hand-painted Tribal Flame graphics.

For the second edition of this model, the CVO motorcycle pulled out the stops in honor of Harley-Davidson's 105th anniversary. The 2008 Screamin' Eagle Softail Springer motorcycle again blended modern performance with nostalgic styling. Attention was again given to overall balance, bringing on 18-inch Revolver wheels front and rear, placing a 130mm tire on the front, and maintaining the 200 on the back. If the front wheel looks more sanitary, it's not just because of the size change: the brake assembly has been moved to the other side of the wheel, too. Further addressing lines and proportion, there's an updated front fender with a newly designed bracket and strut to amp up the bike's attitude. As before, the ergonomically scooped-out seat brings the rider just 24.5 inches off the ground, while forward controls and drag-style handlebars aid rider comfort and confidence.

The Twin Cam 110B engine returns, properly decked out in granite powder-coating, but the big news is the free-flowing Heavy Breather intake providing a 5 percent jolt in torque that tops out at 110 foot pounds at 3,000 RPM. The forward-facing, hot rod air cleaner adds a jolt in the looks department, too, boosting the perfect mix of engineering and custom class so at home on the Springer motorcycle. Word is, the former race-only intake was reengineered for the street in the CVO motorcycle skunk works, totally justifying the "110 c.i." badge it wears with authority.

Also new: a floating rear brake caliper, fuel pump, plus bolt-on frame inserts and fender support covers. Centerline accessories stay put, including the addition of a horn cover, and braided cables and lines come on board.

In 2008, Harley-Davidson called this hue Inferno Orange with Fireburst flames.

Further refinements in cohesive color and graphics make the 2008 Softail Springer motorcycle look seamless. The effect begins on the front fender and headlight bucket, then continues to the rear fender. Kicking it up, metal grind accents return, this time in a new flame-like pattern, coated in transparent candy for maximum pop. Color options for 2008: Inferno Orange with Fireburst Flames; Black Diamond with Smoked Candy Flames; and the exquisite 105th Anniversary Crystal Copper and Black Onyx with gold leafing graphics and a serialized 105th Anniversary cloisonné badge.

As we saw in the discussion of the Screamin' Eagle Ultra Classic Electra Glide motorcycle, "Screamin' Eagle" was finally replaced with "CVO" for model names in the program's tenth anniversary year. The 2009 FXSTSSE CVO Softail Springer motorcycle returned for its third consecutive year in familiar powertrain trim: the granite powder-coated, chrome-covered 110 cubic inch Twin Cam engine is again clad in the much-admired Heavy Breather air intake and mated to a six-speed Cruise Drive transmission. As the largest displacement package available, it provides more than enough get-up-and-go.

Road Winder chrome-forged aluminum wheels replace the Revolvers in stunning style. Up front there's a 130mm radial and a fresh four-piston front caliper with new forged chrome mount. A wider than ever 240mm radial rolls out back, necessitating a new, bobbed rear fender as well.

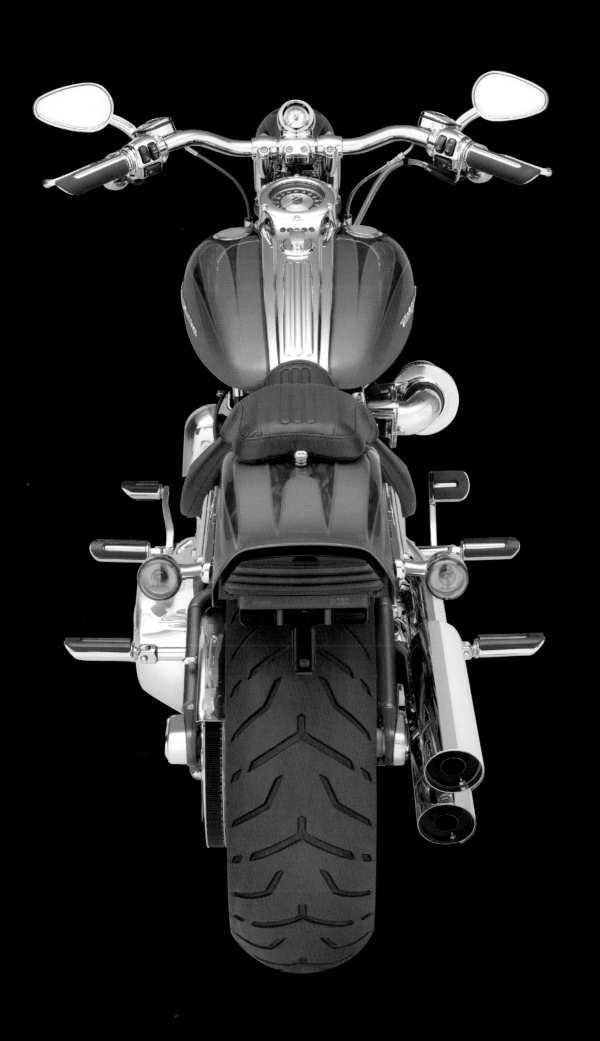

RIGHT:
In 2009 Harley-Davidson offered the CVO Springer Softail motorcycle with Candy Cobalt paint highlighted by Blue Steel flames.

Two paint schemes—Diamond Black with Emerald Ice Flames and Candy Cobalt with Blue Steel Flames—blatantly show off metal grind accents amid scalloped flames on their tanks. The third, Sunrise Yellow Pearl with Volcanic Fury Flames, furtively hides its grind under transparent candy, begging for a closer look.

Recognizing the inherent anti-dive tendencies of a Springer front end, *American Motorcyclist*'s Richard Ried said of the Springer motorcycle, "Between the near-perfect ergonomics, solid handling and that retro-cool front end that really works, the Springer is a bike that is as much fun to ride as it is to look at."

That, in a nutshell, sums up the CVO Softail Springer motorcycle.

Classic Americana incarnate: the CVO Springer Softail.

Another option for 2009 was Black Diamond with Emerald Ice flames.

FLSTSE CVO SOFTAIL CONVERTIBLE MODEL

Over Harley-Davidson's long and varied model history, there have been convertible-style motorcycles built on several platforms. The FXR Convertible and Dyna Convertible models come to mind. As their names imply, both were based on the idea that one motorcycle, with or without modular touring trim, could fulfill the job of two separate motorcycles. With saddlebags and windshield, it's fit to pack and go. Stripped down to bare essentials, it's a boulevard cruiser poised to profile. The concept is the best bargain in motorcycling, two bikes for the price of one.

But it was well into the 2000s before a Harley-Davidson Softail motorcycle was graced with the Convertible designation, and that was due to the CVO motorcycle program.

From the start of the Harley-Davidson factory custom concept, CVO models had seldom been promoted as bargains—that was hardly the point. But with the CVO Softail Convertible motorcycle, you actually *did* get two bikes for one price. That was the intent of a convertible motorcycle, after all. In the case of the CVO Softail Convertible motorcycle, customers could boast of having *two* exquisitely embellished, high-performance bikes. I'd call that *quite* a bargain.

The 2010 CVO Softail Convertible motorcycle bares its ape hangers.

And there was no better time for a bargain, either. As much as the CVO line remained bulletproof when motorcycle sales started dropping during the economic downturn a year or so before, there were still practical matters to be considered. It's true: CVO motorcycle buyers are different from other motorcycle buyers; in fact they're different from other Harley-Davidson motorcycle buyers. Discerning is a word some use, particular is another. Research has shown that people who buy CVO models often plan the purchase for years and follow through when the time is right for them, external circumstances aside. So even these faithful, "aspirational" buyers, as they've been termed, liked the idea of getting twice the bike for one price. Who wouldn't? But that didn't mean they wanted less than a top-of-the-line product.

So as Harley-Davidson's paint and graphic artists had done 75 times by 2010, they once again conceived and executed even more new ways to make sheet metal distinctive, this time for the Convertible motorcycle. The CVO Softail Convertible

Dark tones make the chrome shine that much brighter.

motorcycle stepped out in Inferno Orange with Vivid Black and Silver Braze Graphics; Abyss Blue with Sapphire and Silver Braze Graphics; and Crimson Red Sunglo with Autumn Haze and Black Candy Grind. Metal grind accents had debuted on the 2006 Fat Boy motorcycle, then returned on several other models as the design team felt appropriate. Don't forget, all of these paint and graphic schemes are hand-applied, one at a time, meriting the attention and praise that the CVO motorcycle team justly receives for such exceptional efforts.

In full dress, the Screamin' Eagle Convertible motorcycle looks tour ready with saddlebags, passenger pillion, and backrest, plus a compact fairing with tinted windshield. Of course, these are all tool-free detachable components; when the owner pops them off, the bike becomes a solo-seated cruiser whose hidden shock, that stealthy trait of all Softail models, leaves people on street corners wondering if that was an old-school hardtail that just passed by. Brilliant!

The engine's low-end grunt and throaty exhaust tone do nothing to dispel this thought either, though it's a fact that no street-going Shovelhead ever took to the turnpike with a 110 cubic inch engine. Harley-Davidson's reliable counterbalanced Twin Cam engine produces a steady 110 foot pounds of torque at 3,000 RPM, H-D's heftiest factory powertrain in 2010. It's matched to a six-speed Cruise Drive transmission that was updated with a new helical-cut fifth gear, a welcome improvement.

Switching between the convertible motorcycle's two personalities is easy for the owner, and that's due to solid planning by the CVO motorcycle team. It's an interesting and gratifying exercise, going through the steps to transform the Convertible. Let's take a long look and a walk through.

When the touring parts are present, there's a natural symmetry to the motorcycle. Its smoke-tinted windshield and paint-matched compact fairing lead your eye to the lines of the fuel tank, stopping for a gander at the substantial granite-powder-coated powerplant and super-slammed leather saddle, the lowest in the lineup at 24.4 inches. Note the subtle buffalo hide inserts here that match those on the passenger pillion, backrest, and paneled saddlebags. Lowered rear suspension, compared to production Softail motorcycles, contributes to the overall road-hugging effect. It's not only a cohesive package stem to stern, but it's a stunner with all the right eye candy. Function is icing on the cake.

In cruising trim, it's another story. The fairing and windshield offer sufficient wind protection, so you'll notice when they're gone. But something else you'll notice are the clean, uncluttered, and sparking lines of the chubby, tapered fork tubes, the chrome risers, and the shiny simplicity of the hand controls and instrumentation. A new digital speedometer/analog tachometer combo gets rave reviews, not only for its raised-up, easier-to-read position, but for its function as well; the spiffy design places digital speed readout at the center and RPM in a sweeping arm around the outside edge—cool. It's nicely nested into the tank console, which is garnished with a spot of color and set off further with chrome detail.

Now, it's also more apparent how the FL-style front fender brings weight and substance forward, all the better to balance the wide, tire-hugging rear fender, which becomes much more visible with the passenger seat gone and saddlebags removed. That absence also highlights a new light bar out back, incorporating stop, turn, and taillights. No visible shocks interrupt the lines, thanks to the Softail chassis. What

Earth tones compliment this sleek, hand-crafted machine.

The CVO Convertible Softail motorcycle adds touring capabilities to the custom formula.

Your CVO motorcycle might help lead you to a new favorite spot.

about the hardware left behind when components are removed? Just two small pegs on each strut and one on each side of the fork.

And now you really notice the sharp styling of the chrome Stinger cast aluminum wheels, 18-inchers front and rear. Chrome sprocket and floating brake rotors match, of course. And look how the color-matched frame works to hold the bike together, cohesively joining fenders, fuel tank, oil tank, and forward-frame downtube with the proper points of color. As CVO motorcycle team manager Jeff Smith said when the 2010 version was released, the CVO Softail Convertible motorcycle was built "to get there in comfort and strip down to style." It works, this motorcycle, in either configuration, and it looks commandingly awesome either way, too. How satisfying.

More than looks, though, is the easy function of switching between setups. It's obvious that engineering took special care here to ensure that the detachable parts worked as beautifully as they look, and they do. A couple of practice sessions and you've got it down pat. That's the kind of standout quality a CVO model offers; laced with luscious chrome, sure, but also infused with pragmatic, purposeful functionality. Other features of note on the bike are a 200/50R18 radial rear tire, high-performance clutch with hydraulic actuation, Ventilator air cleaner, and chromed-out shorty dual exhaust with slashdown mufflers and heat shields.

The following year brought the introduction of the second of three CVO Convertible motorcycles in a row. Like its predecessor, the 2011 iteration featured easily detachable components that netted the owner double duty from one motorcycle. The windshield, fairing, saddlebags, and passenger seat with backrest stay in place when light touring is in store, all to be left in the garage for one-up drifting. But that description misses the drama for 2011 because this model broke the mold for Softail motorcycles

Easily removable saddlebags give the CVO Convertible Softail motorcycle serious luggage capacity.

LEFT:
The CVO motorcycle owner's favorite spot to relax.

BELOW:
Layers and shades you could fall right into.

in several ways. According to Terry Roorda, reviewing the model in *Thunder Press*, "In many fundamental ways it's the breakout model of the year."

Prime among the upgrades—and a first for Softail motorcycles—is electronic throttle control technology, replacing mechanical control with far quicker electronics. This results in better throttle response, and riders find that ABS and cruise control operation on this model are super easy. Remaining wiring runs through new retro-looking handlebars, cleaning up the looks.

The much-lauded, high-tech speedometer/tachometer combo returns, with backlit face and spun-metal detailing. The Convertible motorcycle is the only Harley model that can brag of this feature. It's also the first Softail motorcycle equipped with a sound system: the 3.5-inch speakers and 20-watt amp are housed in the fairing, plus there's a dock for an MP3 player.

There are redesigned roomier saddlebags that are easier to get in and out of, and they lock. A selection of bolt-ons from H-D's Parts & Accessories Rumble Collection found a home on the Convertible motorcycle in 2014, and they make a return in the current year's model. Thin ribbons of chrome alternate with black sections, adding flash and function to grips, floorboards, passenger and shifter pegs, brake pedal pad, and mirrors.

New colors and graphics took the stage on this model in the form of three new combinations: Maple Metallic and Roman Gold with Burnished Copper Graphics; Midnight Sky and Candy Cobalt with Blue Ice Graphics; and Scarlet Red Pearl and Dark Slate Pearl with Metal Grind Graphics, a raw metal treatment of perennial high appeal.

For the 2012 FLSTSE Softail Convertible motorcycle, Harley-Davidson's CVO motorcycle team kept rider comfort squarely front and center with a new detachable fairing and a taller, wider windscreen. Why? Because customers asked for it and Harley-Davidson is a customer led company. Venting and adjustable lower wind deflectors made the cut, too. This model year also maintained the Convertible motorcycle's comfortable ergonomics with low seat height, upright seating position, and relaxed reach to the bars. Tech-savvy riders appreciated the new Garmin 660 with integrated MP3 player, audio system, onboard Smart Security System, and ABS.

Improving function, the detachable saddlebags now seal tighter and are lockable, but that's only half the story. Addressing looks, as we know the CVO motorcycle team always does, the styling guys designed the bags in distressed brown leather for the Satin Pewter paint scheme, and reptile inserts for the others. It looks marvelous! The same treatments go on the custom seat and removable passenger pillion/backrest, so everything matches, naturally. There's even leather trim on the Ventilator air cleaner.

ABOVE:
Harley-Davidson gave its Convertible Softail model the CVO motorcycle treatment for the 2010 model year.

OPPOSITE TOP:
The naked truth: a 2011 CVO Softail Convertible motorcycle in stripped-down cruising trim.

OPPOSITE BOTTOM:
Custom touches like these tall, internally wired bars set CVO machines apart.

BELOW:

Harley-Davidson motorcycles are steeped in tradition, but the CVO motorcycle team don't hesitate to add modern functionality.

ABOVE:

For 2011 Harley-Davidson added Scarlet Red Pearl and Dark Slate Pearl with Metal Grind graphics to the CVO Softail Convertible's motorcycle color palate.

And, oh yes, those paint schemes: Crimson Red Sunglo with Scarlet Crystal Graphics; Abyss Blue with Catacomb Graphics; and Satin Pewter with Catacomb Graphics.

Touring couldn't be easier than this, aided by the air-cooled Twin Cam 110B engine with electronic Sequential Port Fuel Injection. Smooth, positive shifting is available, compliments of the standard six-speed Cruise Drive transmission and assisted by the hydraulic-actuated high-performance clutch.

So, as the ultimate bargain of biking, giving the owner two motorcycles for the price of one, how does the CVO Softail Convertible motorcycle complete its mission? Ask someone who owns one: CVO motorcycle owners love to talk about their motorcycles. We think they'll tell you that, whether set up as a minimalist, hardtail-looking cruiser or as a fat-featured high-tech tourer, the FLSTSE Softail Convertible motorcycle handles either duty with style, grace, and superb functionality. Because it does.

In 2010 Harley-Davidson offered the CVO Convertible Softail motorcycle in Abyss Blue and Sapphire with Silver Braze graphics (top), Inferno Orange and Vivid Black with Silver Braze graphics (center), and Crimson Red Sunglo and Autumn Haze with Metal Grind graphics (bottom).

FXSBSE BREAKOUT: THE COOLEST CVO SOFTAIL MODEL YET

The appropriately named Breakout motorcycle lived up to its name from the start: see, it became a CVO model even *before* it was a production bike, the first-ever CVO model adapted for production *after* the fact. This was also the first time that Harley-Davidson engineers and designers from both the custom and production sides collaborated on a new model, noteworthy in itself. In fact, the CVO Breakout motorcycle broke the mold in so many ways, we'll probably forget to mention some of them.

Released in August of 2012 to replace the CVO Softail Convertible motorcycle of previous years, the 2013 CVO Breakout motorcycle garnered immediate attention in force from both media outlets and regular riders. It was quickly compared to the first-ever CVO Softail motorcycle, the trailblazing '03 Deuce model. And that's not a bad thing, considering the Deuce motorcycle's raked front end, sexy lines, and distinct front and rear wheel sizes. The Breakout motorcycle soon built up comparable devotion from owners, too, gaining its own Facebook page and a hefty presence on CVO motorcycle forums.

What's so captivating about the Breakout motorcycle? Plenty, and it starts with styling. With its low, long, slammed profile, the bike was described by *TopSpeed* as "one of the purest representations of a classic American motorcycle." Chopper cues are present not only in the raked front end but also in the fenders, which have been bobbed to the legal limits to expose a bigger chunk of tire on both ends. With discernible muscle car character, the tall 21-inch front wheel blends with a meaty 240mm rear tire and braided steel vent lines. An abundance of chrome is perfectly proper here, too.

Seeing is believing.

And that's the way they planned it. According to Harley-Davidson Styling Manager Kirk Rasmussen, the Breakout motorcycle was intended to project a tough attitude, one that began by stripping the motorcycle down to the essentials and continued forward while keeping that bare-bones vision firmly in mind.

To that end, perhaps no other model showcases the Twin Cam 110B engine as its jewel in the crown quite as well as the Breakout motorcycle. An aggressive cruiser like this naturally sports Harley's largest displacement V-twin engine, displacing 110 cubic inches and pounding out an astonishing 112 pound feet of peak torque. Mated to the smooth and quiet six-speed Cruise Drive transmission, low-RPM cruising could not feel any more capable, the presence of raw power on demand could not be more assured.

As purists will tell you, a motorcycle's essentials are an engine and two wheels, so proper attention was given to the Breakout motorcycle's rolling stock. Brand-new Chrome Turbine cast aluminum wheels made their debut here—exclusive to this model. Sculpted spokes that meet the rim in curved perfection are given grace to shine. The tall 21-inch wheel and generously spaced spokes add visual lightness to the front end, further aided by assertive rake. That muscle-bound 240mm rear tire wraps an 18-inch Turbine rear wheel—with coordinated sprocket and rotor, of course.

In recent years, the rolling stock on CVO machines has defied description.

OPPOSITE TOP LEFT:
Custom badging shines brighter in the sunlight.

OPPOSITE TOP RIGHT:
"CVO" means turning the necessary into the exquisite.

OPPOSITE BOTTOM:
Big wheels dominate big vistas.

BELOW:
Nothing is safe from being customized on a CVO motorcycle!

ABOVE:
Every inch of a CVO motorcycle shows the talent of its makers.

When you consider the Breakout motorcycle's low center of gravity and the fact that it has the best power-to-weight ratio of any model in the CVO lineup to this point, the CVO Breakout motorcycle's appeal makes total sense. Know, too, that inspiration for the Breakout motorcycle came from people like you: the Harley-Davidson customer, the aftermarket brain trust, and dealer input. That's because the Motor Company has always wisely monitored trends, watching to see how customers customized their bikes, then listening to feedback. That's often been the genesis of new models over the decades, and the Breakout motorcycle is a textbook example of this phenomenon.

It started with the Rocker model, released in 2008. With its raked front end, 240mm rear tire and slammed, swing-arm-mounted rear fender, the Rocker motorcycle took a stand. As it filtered into the aftermarket and was altered, mainly with a more classic rear fender, the Rocker motorcycle revealed the demand for a traditional Softail model custom. H-D recognized this: while their designers captured the proper look, engineers devised a way to mate the 110 engine to that big 240 rubber. Thus was born what might be the best-selling H-D Softail motorcycle to date, the Breakout model. Brought to you by the Rocker motorcycle —and the V-twin motorcycle aftermarket.

CVO models always excel when it comes to paint and graphics, and the Breakout motorcycle is no exception. But in addition to the canvas being expanded by trimming the bike's console tighter than any preceding model, a new paint technique unique to production motorcycles was applied this year. The hand-polished metal paint features lace effects for a dazzling shine that just won't quit. Three options took the stage: Black Diamond and Molten Silver with Crushed Slate Graphics; Crimson Red Sunglo and Scarlet Lace with Hammered Sterling Graphics; and the premium metal-flake Hard Candy Gold Dust and Liquid Sun with Pagan Gold Graphics, bringing back the psychedelic 1970s in one bold statement.

OPPOSITE TOP:

The CVO Breakout motorcycle is all about contrast, from spoke to saddle.

OPPOSITE BOTTOM:

There have never been this many shades of grey.

Extra rake in the frame gives the CVO Breakout motorcycle its commanding profile.

Added rider comfort came in the form of new-for-2013 Slipstream Controls that offered a lighter, smoother touch to shifter, hand grips, and brake pedal—all characteristics appropriate to a premium custom bike. But getting back to the Breakout motorcycle's true mission, as *Motorcycle USA's* Brian Harley stated succinctly: "The Breakout features styling that's smooth, tight, and intended to showcase the engine and the tires."

And that sums up the 2013 CVO Breakout motorcycle. There was no better time to break the rules with a head-turning, tasty supermodel of a motorcycle than in the Motor Company's 110th year, or to celebrate the CVO motorcycle program's 15th anniversary year. And actually beating the production model to the market, too? Yeah, that definitely describes the 2013 CVO Breakout motorcycle.

To say the CVO Breakout motorcycle was slightly less true to its moniker in the 2014 model year because it *retained* most of its striking attributes would be like claiming Cindy Crawford was less beautiful at 25 than she was at 24. The Breakout motorcycle lost absolutely *nothing* in its 2014 iteration, once again surpassing expectations whether rolling or standing still. Its long and low mission stays solid with that skinny 21-inch front wheel and 130mm tire paired with a 240mm rear. Chopped fenders and raked front end make for sleek, slammed styling that turns heads—and kicks up dust—everywhere it goes. And, by the way, those Contrast Chrome Turbine custom wheels are unique to this year's model exclusively, their artfully designed negative space adding visual lightness that translates more as a feeling than a thought.

More than 30 years on, the Softail motorcycle benefits from the CVO motorcycle team treatment.

The CVO Breakout motorcycle in solo-saddle mode

The CVO Breakout motorcycle was so popular it was brought into the standard H-D catalogue.

The Screamin' Eagle Twin Cam 110B powerplant retains the granite powder-coated finish and 110 branding. It's mounted in Harley-Davidson's vaunted Softail chassis, whose coil-over shocks, hidden within the frame rails, link rider, and machine in a duet that rewards body English and aggressive participation with fluid motion and outstanding handling. Some call it a cruiser, but cruising behind these bars will only get you a ride; engaging with the bike, on the other hand, will net you a peg-dragging experience. And the Breakout motorcycle was built for this kind of connection with its rider.

There are three new paint options for 2014: Molten Silver and Black Diamond with Forged Iron Graphics; Candy Cobalt and Molten Silver with Abyss Blue Graphics; and Hard Candy Sedona Sand and Blaze Orange with Abyss Blue Graphics. For those riders lucky enough to snag a 2014 CVO Breakout motorcycle, their only dilemma was, which one?

Also new for 2014 are the Bomber black leather seat, featuring tribal embossed panels, chrome fuel tank medallions, and the epic, elbow-styled Screamin' Eagle Heavy Breather air cleaner. Its Screamin' Eagle 110 insert broadcasts hot-rod cues, and the engine totally lives up to the hype with performance.

Returning are all the other accoutrements from the 2013 that make the Breakout motorcycle the premium custom motorcycle it is: abundant chrome details, ABS, Slipstream controls, hydraulic clutch, and H-D Factory Security System. The perfect storm of inspiration and engineering.

Details with dimension.

Long and low, the unique wheels jump out in profile.

The 2014 CVO Softail Deluxe motorcycle captures the looks of a 1950s-era touring motorcycle, except that 1950s-era touring motorcycles never looked this good.

FLSTNSE
CVO SOFTAIL
DELUXE MODEL

How do you doll up a motorcycle that's already called the "Deluxe?" The right people for *that* job work in Harley-Davidson's CVO motorcycle department, and you better believe they're up to the task. Briefly put, as a premium custom touring machine, the Softail Deluxe motorcycle features long-haul capacity and CVO motorcycle styling. But like any model in the 16-year history of Harley-Davidson's custom vehicle operations, this characterization barely skims the surface.

Coming into the H-D production model lineup in 2005, the Softail Deluxe motorcycle took the stage as a "CVO" moniker for the first time in 2014. It was called by one reviewer "a Rockabilly Dream," while another termed it "a Modern Classic." Said Florida radio DJ and avid rider Rick Stacey, "The engineers and designers at Harley found a way to wrap quintessential classic Harley styling around an array of new technology."

The Deluxe model was always a motorcycle that excelled in nostalgic styling with its wide whitewalls, FL-style fenders, and roomy floorboards. Those same classic design touchstones come along to the CVO model, ramped up to superior specifications as you'd expect in any motorcycle bearing the CVO moniker. Chrome nine-spoke cast aluminum wheels replace the production model's laced ones. Art deco cues in the paint scheme also lend a certain stately feel, bolstered by a slew of touring components that stir a rider's desire to quickly pack up a few things and point the bike's front tire down a two-lane blacktop.

That was actually part of the plan with the CVO Softail Deluxe motorcycle. It was equipped for touring with lockable, detachable saddlebags and a detachable windscreen with an integrated Road Tech Zumo 660 GPS Navigator. There's a luggage rack, sissy bar, and passenger pad as well, equipping the motorcycle for the long haul. But here's the clincher: all of these components pop off with relative ease, so when you get where you're going you can lighten the load for a spin around town. Aiding highway visibility is Daymaker LED lighting awash in chrome. The Mustache engine guard is equipped with footpads, encouraging the rider to stretch out and go the distance.

Echoes of the '50s and '60s abound in profile.

Remember the good ol' days with the power
and reliability to ride into the future.

Nostalgic charm with a healthy dose of modern power and luxury.

But let's talk about handling, because this is where styling and engineering joined forces to imbue the Softail Deluxe motorcycle with particular attributes. In a beautiful balance of form and function, this motorcycle's low center of gravity, 24-inch seat height, and pullback handlebars allow the rider to tackle the road with confidence, especially for those of smaller stature. Further enhancing rider assurance is Harley-Davidson's long-exalted Softail chassis with its rear suspension control, provided by hidden coil-over shocks mounted between the frame rails. Add to these qualities the unrelenting power and gobs of low-end torque available thanks to the Screamin' Eagle Twin Cam 110B motor and the result is a solid connection between rider and machine. The ultimate experience in low-RPM cruising.

As the Motor Company's largest displacement OE engine, the Screamin' Eagle Twin Cam 110B engine is only offered in CVO motorcycles. Granite-finished heads and cylinders dovetail with machined fins. Chrome rocker covers add just enough shine and 110 badging on the high-flow Ventilator performance air cleaner leaves no question about the power on board. With 110 foot pounds of torque at 3,750 RPM, Softail Deluxe motorcycle riders won't be left wanting for get-up-and-go, especially when set up for day-cruising mode. Expect smooth, quiet shifting from the six-speed Cruise Drive transmission. According to Harley-Davidson's literature, it reduces engine speed on the highway for a better match between engine RPM and road speed.

The other side of going is stopping, and there's state-of-the-art componentry in that department on the Softail Deluxe motorcycle as well, thanks to dual-disc Brembo brakes. Four-piston calipers, front and rear, mate with the single front rotor brake system for top-notch performance. And, yes, ABS is on board; the mechanical components are integrated into the design to maintain the motorcycle's styling cues.

Do you see the attraction of the Deluxe model?

The first iteration of the CVO Softail Deluxe motorcycle was offered in three paint schemes, each resplendent with Airflow Graphics: Crimson Red Sunglo and Ruby Red; Candy Cobalt and White Gold Pearl; and Maple Metallic and Atomic Orange. There's a refined geometric feel to the design, contemporary art deco, if you will.

For its encore performance in 2015, the Softail Deluxe motorcycle returned with gusto, packing everything it was praised for in 2014 and more. Accolades flowed over convenience components such as electronic cruise control, keyless ignition, and the H-D Factory Security System. The easy-reach sidestand was redesigned for quicker access, and lighter clutch lever effort thanks to easy actuation of the hydraulic clutch is a favorite feature, too. Another bonus is the slip feature on the Assist & Slip Clutch Pack, a trait that's both rider- and driveline-friendly.

The front brakes were treated to an upgrade with a new four-piston fixed caliper up front, featuring larger pistons and premium piston coating. Combined with a redesigned master cylinder and 300mm front rotor, the system provides superior braking control—again with reduced lever effort.

The 2015 CVO Softail Deluxe motorcycle is touring-ready at the drop of a hat, whenever the wind changes or the whim takes you, with quick-detach windshield, saddlebags, luggage rack, backrest, and passenger pillion. Or simply cruise the boulevard in retro style, feet firmly on the wide floorboards while white sidewalls roll along elegantly under classically styled FL fenders. The Softail chassis won't reveal the secret that it's *not* actually a vintage hardtail.

A generous selection of components from the Slipstream Collection were plucked from the H-D Parts & Accessories Catalog. Parts in this line contrast rubber and chrome sections in angular counterpoint to coincidentally match the model's curvy, lush paint motif. Bolted on for service from the Slipstream line are narrow grips, shifter pegs, brake pedal pad, footboards, passenger pegs, and much more.

As for the paintwork, its clean, swirling graphics and artful tank badging enhance the sheet-metal lines in the CVO model's usual opulent fashion. We've really become spoiled, haven't we? Owners could choose from Bermuda Blue and Stardust Silver or Black Crystal and Dark Tungsten.

Looking for a motorcycle that meets modern technology head on while keeping Harley-Davidson heritage firmly in mind? The Softail Deluxe motorcycle does it all.

Every angle contains a reference to Harley-Davidson history.

CHAPTER 5

At the end of the day, all CVO motorcycles are built for riders: here, H-D's Mike Kull speaks with a lifetime HOG member about the 2006 VRSCSE2 model.

V-ROD MOTORCYCLES: PERFORMANCE WITH A CAPITAL V

VRSCSE SCREAMIN' EAGLE V-ROD MODEL

The Screamin' Eagle V-Rod motorcycle devours another stretch of asphalt.

When you think of CVO Harley-Davidson motorcycles, one word instantly springs to mind: exclusivity. Custom touches from the company that invented the concept, layered carefully on modern engineering with a rock-solid respect for history, add up to everything CVO machines are bred to. But among the wide range of machines the factory has rolled out of its York, Pennsylvania, CVO skunk works, the VRSCSE Screamin' Eagle V-Rod motorcycle stands apart—and not only because it was produced at Harley-Davidson's Kansas City Vehicle and Powertrain Operations facility. Produced for just two years in 2005 and 2006, CVO V-Rod motorcycles reigned supreme with their powerful 1,250cc Revolution engines, then unique to CVO machines.

The 2005 Screamin' Eagle V-Rod motorcycle came in two-tone Candy Cherry (top), Candy Blue and Dark Candy Blue (center), and Electric Orange and Black (bottom).

Even with that distinction, the V-Rod motorcycle has always been a motorcycle with two personalities. First and foremost, it's a Harley-Davidson motorcycle, dripping with the quality, independence, and panache the brand has upheld for more than a century. But since its introduction as a production bike in 2001, it's also been the motorcycle that carried Harley-Davidson into the twenty-first century, with its race-developed Revolution engine, extensive use of lightweight aluminum, and aggressive stance and styling. The V-Rod motorcycle dared to set the pace for the *next* hundred years.

It was inevitable that Harley-Davidson would eventually bless its distinctive new model with exclusive CVO motorcycle treatment. The first few years of V-Rod motorcycle production produced a strong following. A "power cruiser" in the purest sense of the phrase, the V-Rod motorcycle modern powerplant and cutting-edge construction introduced a whole new population of motorcyclists to the unique sensation of riding a genuine Harley-Davidson motorcycle. The styling of the V-Rod motorcycle was a departure, though, with a muscle-bound look highlighted by the V-Rod motorcycle's advanced hydroformed aluminum perimeter frame. But it's also a powerful advancement; more than a decade on from the initial unveiling, the V-Rod motorcycle has become a modern classic in its own right.

But what's a bike that's all show with no go? That's not a dilemma the V-Rod motorcycle contended with. Compared to the more traditional models in the lineup, the Screamin' Eagle V-Rod motorcycle had a serious ace up its sleeve: the liquid-cooled and fuel-injected, four-stroke, 60-degree V-Twin Revolution engine. Many of the lessons learned from Harley's VR-1000 road racing machine were applied during the development of the Revolution engine. By the time the fearsome powerplant had been cradled in the V-Rod motorcycle's color-matched, powder-coated frame for the street, its distinctive V-twin howl had been heard on road courses around the world.

CVO motorcycle engineers managed to squeeze even more power from the mighty Revolution motor.

To any classically trained member of the Harley faithful, the spec sheet raises more than a few eyebrows: Twin overhead cams, liquid cooling, and internal counterbalancing are modern features, all the more impressive for their first appearance in a century of motorcycles from Milwaukee. Even the 45-degree V configuration that's so beautiful and familiar has been stretched out to 60 degrees. But in the pursuit of ultimate usable power, flexibility, and refinement, compromise wasn't an option. Development work involved input from Porsche, a company with almost as rich a history as Harley-Davidson itself. But, more importantly, Porsche's powerplants were traditionally air-cooled, before the company gradually developed liquid-cooling technology as the need for more power and refinement became apparent; perhaps a path to emulate.

VRSCSE motorcycle riders need not want for power *or* refinement thanks to careful development and tuning. The Revolution powerplant in the Screamin' Eagle V-Rod motorcycle spins up to a mighty 9,000 RPM redline, leaving a pavement-melting 123 horsepower in its wake. The location chosen for the CVO model release to moto-journalists in 2005 could not have been more fitting for the Screamin' Eagle V-Rod motorcycle: the Irwindale Dragstrip near Los Angeles, where press reps got to thwack open the throttle down the eighth-mile strip on the new CVO models—to rousing acclaim!

That extra power takes careful cultivation, including CNC ported heads, studious tweaks to the camshaft timing, as well as punching the displacement out from 69 cubic inches to 76, all in the name of pleasure on two wheels. "Wind the engine up to the redline and make short work of the next quarter mile and beyond!" said Cyril Demortier on *TopSpeed.com*. This motor proved so successful that production V-Rod motorcycles adopted this more powerful motor after the VRSCSE model bowed at the end of 2006.

V-Rod power meets exclusivity with the VRSCSE CVO model.

But, like every CVO model, it's not *just* about power. Head-turning paint schemes and graphic treatments are always in the mix, and the Screamin' Eagle V-Rod motorcycle is no exception. The 2005 VRSCSE model debuted in the brand-stamped Electric Orange and Black familiar to every Screamin' Eagle motorcycle fan. Two additional two-tone combinations were available, including Light Candy Blue with Dark Candy Blue, and Light Candy Cherry with Dark Candy Cherry. A quick tip for would-be VRSCSE motorcycle spotters: all Screamin' Eagle V-Rod motorcycles had their frames powder-coated to match the unique color of the bodywork.

The wheels were unique pieces, too. Simultaneously classic and perfectly modern, the five-spoke Reactor wheels frame the bike splendidly. This custom rolling stock features a brilliant chrome finish, as well as svelte spokes that invoke the look of classic Invader mag wheels from the 1970s. The rear wheel is wide enough to take a meaty 180mm tire while keeping the back end of the bike tight and coherent. Power is transmitted to the rear wheel via a matching Reactor rear pulley.

Every custom bike fan knows you can't speak custom without talking chrome. While certainly not new to CVO machines, nothing says class and power quite like high-quality chrome accessories—and the VRSCSE model has an appropriately heaping helping. From the bucket and shroud surrounding the projector-beam headlight up front to the swingarm and muffler end caps at the back, chrome is comfortably at home here. Even more practical components pulled from the Harley-Davidson Genuine Motor Parts & Genuine Motor Accessories Catalog gleam with the shiny stuff, such as the hand and foot controls, sidestand, and the braided stainless steel control cables, clutch, and brake lines. The 1.25-inch diameter handlebars feature internal wiring, and controls are modified with a new chrome riser, clamp, and bracket that support the speedometer and tachometer. Here you'll find handsome metalwork in the details too; check out the spun aluminum gauge faces, the sort of subtle custom touch that makes CVO models shine, whether you're just walking by or taking a long, slow look.

The second and last year of the VRSCSE model, 2006, brought more treats. The classic orange-and-black paint combination stayed on the menu, but the reds and blues were replaced with the high-contrast Scarlet Red Pearl with Charcoal Slate, as well as Chrome Yellow Pearl with Platinum Pearl. The rear view also grew a little bit, with an even more commanding 240mm rear tire to turn heads and put down the power. And when it was time to slow all those horses down, the 2006 models got the magic touch of Brembo binders and brake discs.

From front to back, the Screamin' Eagle V-Rod motorcycle has the kind of power that few CVO models can touch, as well as the details small and large that define what the Custom Vehicle Operations motorcycle program is all about. But the VRSCSE model is *more* than an impressive CVO Harley-Davidson motorcycle: it's an impressive *motorcycle*.

VRXSC SCREAMIN' EAGLE V-ROD DESTROYER MODEL

By now, it's clear the lengths to which the CVO motorcycle program will go when it comes to impressing the motorcycling public with a piece of exclusive, powerful, fully featured moto-art. But there's another CVO machine that doesn't quite fit even CVO model's unconventional mold. It doesn't have any special paint, it actually had fewer features than the production model it was based upon, and it wasn't even street-legal. Sound like a dog? You've got another thing coming: behold the VRXSC Screamin' Eagle V-Rod Destroyer model.

You're looking at the only factory racing machine Harley-Davidson has produced since the fabled XR-750 motorcycle, the dirt-track weapon that ate AMA Grand National Championships for breakfast and the road race VR1000 motorcycles. It's been more than three decades since you could buy an XR-750 motorcycle, but the VRXSC model takes up the torch with pride and power to boot. Just like the XR-750 motorcycle, if you had the cash and the right racing license, you too could mosey up to your local Harley-Davidson dealership and order one for yourself, an honest-to-iron production race bike, built for one purpose: winning races. It was a brilliant and bold move by the CVO motorcycle team, but not a new idea; Harley-Davidson has been a part of motorcycle racing longer than any other motorcycle company, from hill climbs to drag strips, flat tracks, and road courses.

"Certainly it's a significant part of Harley-Davidson history and a significant part of our (CVO) history," said Jim Hofman. "We are very proud of that bike and the fact that we could really get outside the box with it."

And justifiably so. Winning drag races is no simple feat; it takes careful management of power, timing, and endless practice and development. And yet the CVO motorcycle team put this bike on the pavement after little more than a year of development, unveiling it at Harley-Davidson's dealer show at the end of 2005. It shows dedication and focus, but the results are even more impressive than the process.

First of all, let's throw out some numbers. Think your bike is quick? The VRXSC model delivers the standing quarter mile in under 10 seconds—if your reaction times are up to it and your reflexes are sharp. Pro AHDRA racers nudged the times down to the 9.2-second mark at the bike's unveiling, but these are guys who live on the strip and breathe nitro. For the rest of us, the sensation might be a little foreign, not to mention terrifying. "It's like walking on tiptoes to the brink of Armageddon," said Mark Hoyer of *Cycle World*, who squeezed off a respectable 9.7 at the press unveiling. With this kind of power, you'd be timid, too.

You may have a friend with a turbo bagger or a big-bore Dyna motorcycle, but this is a whole different animal. With its aluminum construction, the Destroyer motorcycle barely tips the scales over 500 pounds, less than a new 883 Sportster motorcycle. Meanwhile, the engine retains the stock crankcases, but the crank is all-new, highly lightened to raise the rev limit and build revs even faster. It's also stroked out to bring the total displacement up to 1300cc at a mind-bending 14:1 compression ratio.

The four valve heads are also special castings, with massive porting work to bring the gas in and out at the staggering rate required by wide-open launches. Tuned fuel injection delivers just the right amount of race fuel, and exhaust thunders out of a huge 2-into-1 header with no baffles or mufflers to speak of. Aggressive cams are in the mix, of course, delivering massive power but requiring the bike to be idled at 2,000 revs! It's all good for 165 horsepower, and nearly 100 foot pounds of torque. A milk run machine this isn't.

Unique for a CVO machine, the Destroyer motorcycle doesn't get points for on-road refinement or rider-friendly features. Every part has one purpose: to devour quarter-mile sections of pavement. So the custom parts you get are all trick speed equipment from around the industry: a high-pressure Pingel air shifter, a data acquisition system for tracking runs and engine performance, and light racing wheels wrapped in drag slicks. Instrumentation is minimal: just three small status lights to distract you from the massive LED shift light. You do get a nice custom seat, like most CVO machines, but on the Destroyer motorcycle it's shaped not for comfort but to keep you from flying off the bike at launch!

While it's a powerful and fearsome machine in every way, it's not numbers that make the V-Rod Destroyer motorcycle important. The essential backstory is Harley-Davidson's return to grass roots racing, such a beloved and significant part of its heritage and a notion that taps right into our American sense of speed and ambition.

V-Rod Destroyer motorcycles may not get treated to the same adornments as other CVO machines, but they do get a special place in history as the motorcycle that put Harley-Davidson racing back on the map. In the words of Jim Hofman, "They're not for everyone, but are there to show what's possible." And on a machine like this, you have to think that anything's possible.

Long, low, and lean: the CVO V-Rod Destroyer motorcycle is nothing if not a race bike.

INDEX